C000138893

# MURDER IN SLOW MOTION

## HOW STALKING RUINED, RULED AND REMADE MY LIFE

### ANNE B SUZA

Britain's Next
**BESTSELLER**

Copyright (C) 2019 by Anne B Suza
All rights reserved.
Published in 2019 by:
Britain's Next Bestseller
An imprint of Live It Ventures LTD
www.bnbsbooks.co.uk
The moral right of Anne B Suza to be identified as the author of this
work has been asserted by her in accordance with the Copyright,
Designs and Patents Act 1988.
Except as permitted under current legislation, no part of this work
may be photocopied, stored in a retrieval system, published,
performed in public, adapted, broadcast, transmitted, recorded or
reproduced in any form or by any means, without the prior
permission of the copyright owners.
All enquiries should be addressed to:
Live It Ventures LTD, 126 Kirkleatham Lane, Redcar. Cleveland.
TS10 5DD


ISBN - 978-190695-4-58-1


Cover design by Miacello©

*I dedicate this book to Suzy and every other victim who has tragically lost their lives to stalking, domestic abuse and cohesive control, not only at the hands of another, but in some cases because they simply could not stand any more.*

I have tried to recreate events, locales and conversations from my memories of them. In order to maintain their anonymity, in some instances, I have changed the names of individuals and places, I may have changed some identifying characteristics and details such as physical properties, occupations and places of residence.

- ANNE B SUZA

I remember the day Suzy Lamplugh went missing.

I always prayed her family would finally have the answers to their questions, but sadly her parents died never knowing what truly happened. Her siblings, friends and former colleagues must think of her daily.

From this tragedy, Diane and Paul Lamplugh set up the Suzy Lamplugh Trust, campaigning tirelessly to raise awareness of personal safety. Without it, who knows how many more lives would have been affected?

# INTRODUCTION
## WHAT IS STALKING?

Stalking involves a person becomes fixated or obsessed with another.

It is a pattern of persistent and unwanted attention that makes you feel pestered, scared, anxious or harassed. Some examples of stalking are:

- Regularly giving unwanted gifts
- Making unwanted communication
- Damaging property
- Repeatedly following you or spying on you
- Threats

Taken in isolation, some of the behaviours may seem like small acts, but together they make up a consistent pattern of behaviour that is frightening and upsetting. It's important to know that stalking is a criminal offence and because of this, if you go to the police they will take it seriously.

## STATISTICS ON STALKING

• A study on the relationship between stalking and homicide involving a female victim and male perpetrator, found that in 71% of cases the victim and perpetrator were in, or had previously had, an intimate relationship [1]

• Data from the Crime Survey of England and Wales shows up to 700, 000 women are stalked each year [2]

• Victims do not tend to report to the police until the 100th Incident [3]

• Statistics show that the majority of victims (80.4%) are female while the majority of perpetrators (70.5%) are male [4]

• The Metropolitan Police Service found that 40% of the victims of domestic homicides had also been stalked [5]

## KEY FACTS AND FIGURES

Stalking is one of the most frequently experienced forms of abuse.

It is insidious and terrifying and can escalate to rape and murder. We need to treat stalking with the seriousness it deserves. There are many misconceptions about what stalking is about. It is not romantic. It is about fixation and obsession. It is a crime. It destroys lives.

Stalking is a pattern of repeat and persistent unwanted behaviour that is intrusive and engenders fear. It is when one person becomes fixated or obsessed with another and the attention is unwanted. Threats may not be made but victims may feel scared. Even if there is no threat this is still stalking and it is a crime.

## FACTS

• Data from the Crime Survey of England and Wales shows up to 700, 000 women are stalked each year (2009-12) although the British Crime Survey (2006) estimated 5 million people experience stalking each year but there are no official statistics on the percentage cyberstalked.

• 1 in 5 women and 1 in 10 men will experience staking in their adult life (*Homicides, Firearm offences and intimate violence 2009/10; Supplementary Volume 2 to Crime in England and Wales 2009/10 2nd Edition. Home Office Statistical Bulletin 01/11*)

• Office for National Statistics (2013) stated it was 1 in 6 women and 1 in 12 men. We still believe this to be grossly underestimated.

• In 2013/14 CPS figures reveal that 743 stalking

offences were prosecuted whereas 9,792 were prose-cuted for harassment out of the 61 175 allegations recorded by police. Therefore only 1% of cases of stalking and 16% of cases of harassment recorded by the police result in a charge and prosecution by the CPS (*Paladin, National Stalking Advocacy Service, 2015*).

• Research reveals that only 11% (n=33) of stalkers received an immediate custodial sentence for Section 2a stalking and just 9% (n=14) for a Section 4a stalking offence in 2013 (*Paladin, National Stalking Advocacy Service, 2015*).

• Victims do not tend to report to the police until the 100th Incident (Sheridan, 2005).

• 50% of victims have curtailed or stopped work due to stalking (Pathe and Mullen 1997)

• The Workplace Violence Research Institute found that 90% of corporate security professionals had handled 3 or more incidents of men stalking women in the workplace and claimed stalking was related to homicide in 15% of cases (Smock and Kuennen, 2002).

• 75% of domestic violence stalkers will turn up at the workplace.

• 79% of domestic violence stalker will use the work resources to target the victims.

• 1 in 2 domestic stalkers, if they make a threat, will

act on it (MacKenzie, McEwan, Pathé, James, Ogloff, & Mullen, 2009).

• 1 in 10 stalkers, who had no prior relationship, if they make a threat will act on it (MacKenzie, McEwan, Pathé, James, Ogloff, & Mullen, 2009).

• Statistics show that the majority of victims (80.4%) are female while the majority of perpetrators (70.5%) are male. (*National Stalking Helpline, 2011*).

• The Metropolitan Police Service found that 40% of the victims of domestic homicides had also been stalked (ACPO Homicide Working Group, 2003).

*Figures supplied by Paladin, the Stalking Advocacy Charity*

## PREFACE

I cannot remember where I found this or who wrote it, but the words are perfect and I kept it all these years for a reason.

 Dear Co-dependent Partner,

What I'm about to say is not something I'd ever say or admit (to you), because to do so would end the *winner-takes-all-game* that is my main source of pleasure in life — one that effectively keeps you carrying my load in our relationship.

And that's the whole point.

When I say "I love you" I mean that I love how hard you work to make me feel like your everything, that I am the focus of your life, that you want me to be happy, and that I'll never be expected to do the same.

I love the power I have to take advantage of your kindness and intentions to be nice, and the pleasure I derive when I make myself feel huge in comparison to you, taking every opportunity to make you feel small and insignificant.

I love the feeling it gives me thinking of you as weak, vulnerable, emotionally fluffy, and I love looking down on you for your childlike innocence and gullibility, as weakness.

I love the way I feel knowing that, through the use of gaslighting, what you want to discuss or address will never happen, and I love this "power" to train you to feel "crazy" for even asking or bringing up issues that don't interest me, effectively, ever lowering your expectations of me and what I'm capable of giving you, while I up mine of you.

I love how easy it is to keep your sole focus on *alleviating my pain (never yours!)* and that, regardless what you do, you'll never make me feel good enough, loved enough, respected enough, appreciated enough, and so on. (Misery loves company.)

(It's not about the closeness, empathy, emotional connection you want, or what I did that hurt or embarrassed you, or how little time I spend engaged with you or the children, and so on. It's about my status and doing my job to keep you in your place, in pain, focused on feeling my pain, blocking you from feeling valued in relation to me. I'm superior and entitled to *all* the pleasure, admiration, and comforting between us, remember?)

"I love you" means I love the way I feel when you are with me, more specifically, regarding you as a piece of property I own, my possession. Like driving a hot car, I love the extent to which you enhance my status in the eyes of others, letting them know that I'm top dog, and so on. I love thinking others are jealous of my possessions.

I love the power I have to keep you working hard to prove your love and devotion, wondering what else you need to do to "prove" your loyalty.

"I love you" means I love the way I feel when I'm with you. Due to how often I hate and look down on others in general, the mirror neurones in my brain keep me constantly experiencing feelings of self-loathing; thus, I love that I can love myself through you, and also love hating you for my "neediness" of having to rely on you or anyone for anything.

I love that you are there to blame whenever I feel this "neediness"; feeling scorn for you seems to protect me from something I hate to admit, that I feel totally dependent on you to "feed" my sense of superiority and entitlement, and to keep my illusion of power alive in my mind.

(Nothing makes me feel more fragile and vulnerable than not having control over something that would tarnish my image and superior status, such as when you question "how" I treat you, as if you still don't understand that getting you to accept yourself as an object for my pleasure, happy regardless of how I treat you, or the children — is key proof of my superiority, to the world. You're my possession, remember? It's my job to teach you to hate and act calloused toward those "crazy" things that only "weak" people need, such as "closeness" and "emotional stuff;" and by the way, I know this "works" because my childhood taught me to do this to myself inside.)

It makes me light up with pleasure (more proof of my superiority) that I can easily get you flustered, make you act "crazy" over not getting what you want from me, make you repeat yourself, and say and do things that you'll later hate yourself for (because of your "niceness"!) Everything you say, any hurts or complaints you share, you can be sure, I'll taunt you with later, to keep you ever-spinning your wheels, ever trying to explain yourself, ever doubting yourself and confused, trying to figure out why I don't "get" it.

(There's nothing to get! To break the code, you'd have to look through my lens, not yours! It's my job to show complete disinterest in your emotional needs, hurts, wants, and to train, dismiss and punish accordingly, until you learn your "lesson," that is: To take your place as a voiceless object, a possession has no desire except to serve my pleasure and comfort, and never an opinion on how its treated!)

(That you can't figure this out, after all the ways I've mistreated you, to me, is proof of my genetic superiority. *In my playbook, those with superior genes are never kind, except to lure and snare their victims!*)

I love that I can make you feel insecure at the drop of a hat, especially by giving attention to other women (perhaps also others in general, friends, family members, children, etc... the list is endless). What power this gives me to put a display of what you don't get from me, to taunt and make you beg for what I easily give to others, wondering why it's so easy to give what you want to others, to express feelings or affection, to give compliments, that is, when it serves my pleasure (in this case, to watch you squirm).

I love the power I have to get you back whenever you threaten to leave, by throwing a few crumbs your way, and watching how quickly I can talk you into trusting me when I turn on the charm, deceiving you into thinking, this time, I'll change.

"I love you" means I need you because, due to the self-loathing I carry inside, I need someone who won't abandon me that I can use as a punching bag, to make myself feel good by making them feel bad about themselves. (This is how I pleasure myself, and the way I numb, deny the scary feelings I carry inside that I hope to never admit, ever. I hate any signs of weakness in me, which is why I hate you, and all those I consider inferior, stupid, feeble, and so on.)

"I love you" means that I love fixing and shaping your thoughts and beliefs, being in control of your mind, so that you think of me as your miracle and saviour, a source of life and sustenance you depend on, and bouncing back to, like gravity, no matter how high you try to fly away or jump.

I love that this makes me feel like a god, to keep you so focused (obsessed…) with making me feel worshiped and adored, sacrificing everything for me to prove yourself so that I don't condemn you, seeking to please none other, and inherently, with sole rights to administer rewards and punishments as I please.

I love how I can use my power to keep

you down, doubting and second-guessing yourself, questioning your sanity, obsessed with explaining yourself to me (and others), professing your loyalty, wondering what's wrong with you (instead of realising that ... *you cannot make someone "happy" who derives their sense of power and pleasure from feeling scorn for others ... and you!*)

"I love you" means I love the way I feel when I see myself through your admiring eyes, that you're my feel-good drug, my dedicated audience, my biggest fan and admirer, and so on. You, and in particular, your looking up to me, unquestionably, as your never-erring, omniscient, omnipotent source of knowledge is *my drug of choice*. (You may have noticed how touchy I am at any signs of being question; yes, I hate how fragile I feel at any sign of thinking that you, or the world, could judge me as having failed to keep my possessions in line.)

And I love that, no matter how hard you beg and plead for my love and admiration, to feel valued in return, it won't happen, as long as I'm in control. Why would I let it, when I'm hooked on deriving pleasure from depriving you of anything that would be wind beneath your wings, risking you'd fly away from me? It gives me great pleasure to *not* give you what you yearn for, the tenderness you need and want, and to burst your every dream and bubble, then telling myself, "I'm no fool."

I love that I can control your attempts to get "through" to me, by controlling your mind, in particular, by shifting the focus of any "discussion" onto what is wrong with you, your failure to appreciate and make me feel loved, good enough — and of course, reminding you of all I've done for you, and how ungrateful you are.

I love how I skilfully manipulate others' opinions of you as well, getting them to side with me as the "good" guy, and side against you as the "bad" guy, portraying you as needy, never satisfied, always complaining, selfish and controlling, and the like.

I love how easy it is for me to say "No!" to what may provide you a sense of value and significance in relation to me, with endless excuses, and that I instead keep your focus on my needs and wants, my discomforts or pain.

I love feeling that I own your thoughts, your ambitions, and ensuring your wants and needs are solely focused on not upsetting me, keeping me happy.

I love being a drug of choice you "have to" have, regardless of how I mistreat you, despite all the signs that your addiction to me is draining the energy from your life, that you are at risk of losing more and more of what you most value, and hold dear, to include the people you love, and those who love and support you.

I love that I can isolate you from others who may nourish you, and break the spell, and I love making you mistrust them, so that you conclude no one else really wants to put up with you, but me.

I love that I can make you feel I'm doing you a favour by being with you and throwing crumbs your way. Like a vacuum, the emptiness inside me is in constant need of sucking the life and breath and vitality you bring to my life, which I crave like a drug that can never satisfy, that I fight to hoard, and hate the thought of sharing.

While I hate you and my addiction to your caring attention, my neediness keeps me craving to see myself through your caring eyes, ever ready to admire, adore, forgive, make excuses for me, and fall for my lies and traps.

I love that you keep telling me how much I hurt you, not knowing that, to me, this is like a free marketing report, which lets me know how effective my tactics have been to keep you in pain, focused on alleviating my pain — so that I am ever the winner in this competition — ensuring that you never weaken (control) me with your love- and emotional-closeness stuff.

In short, when I say "I love you," I love the power I have to remain a mystery that you'll never solve because of what you do not know (and refuse to believe), that: the only one who can win this zero-sum-winner-takes-all game is the one who knows "the rules." My sense of power rests on ensuring you never succeed at persuading me to join you in creating a mutually-kind relationship because, in my worldview, being vulnerable, emotionally expressive, kind, caring, empathetic, innocent are signs of weakness, proof of inferiority.

Thanks, but no thanks, I'm resolved

to stay on my winner-takes-all ground, ever in competition for the prize, gloating in my narcissistic ability to be heartless, callous, cold, calculating … and proud, to ensure my neediness for a sense of superiority isn't hampered.

Forever love-limiting,

Your narcissist

*PS: I really, really need help — but you CANNOT do this work for me (not without making things worse for both of us!). Remember, we're co-addicted to each other, so we'd never go to an addict to get help, right?*

*Only a therapist, with experience in this, stands a chance, and even then, only if I choose to really, really, really let him/her! (That's because I'd have to face my greatest fear that, not only am I not superior to everyone and thus not entitled to make and break rules as I please, but I'd also have to own — that my own actions, thoughts and beliefs about myself and others — are THE main cause of the suffering in my life … and changing them, THE solution. I could not would not ever want to do this for the sole reason that, from my worldview, only the feeble-minded and weak do such things!)*

## [ 1 ]

THE BEGINNING

S<small>INCE</small> <small>SIGNING</small> <small>THE</small> <small>PUBLICATION</small> C<small>ONTRACT</small> <small>FOR</small> Murder in Slow Motion, I have had to literarily re-write most of the book, so the person in question doesn't sue me or the publisher.

What that means is that it has become a very different book to what I first wanted. It was never about me, and it was never about him. We were just bit players in an epidemic that is sweeping the country and, no doubt, the world.

The characteristic traits of a stalker are the same as the domestic abuser and the perpetrators of coercive control. If they don't get their own way, they harass, intimidate and they can be very unpredictable. I suppose that is part of what they would class as their charm.

And charming, they most certainly can be.

I was never in a relationship with mine, not in a romantic relationship anyway. He was the chairman of the company I worked for. I liked and respected him and his family a lot. I didn't like the managing director who was a bully, and I knew my time at the company was coming to an end and I had started looking for alternative employment. But before I found another role, the gates of hell opened.

I was asked if I was having an affair with the married finance director; I wasn't. A few weeks later, he was arrested and his employment terminated, accused of Fraud by Misrepresentation. My employment was then terminated.

For the record, the finance director was eventually charged with Fraud by Misrepresentation and stood trial. The first trial collapsed. At the second trial, the managing director gave evidence and produced evidence that the police and the defence solicitors had repeatedly requested, but to which were denied access.

This is what I received from the chairman.

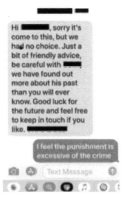

THIS EVIDENCE WAS COPIED, AND THE CPS HAD two weeks to decide if they wanted the trial to continue. They attended Court with the defendant and stated that if they'd had this evidence, they would not have made a charging decision and accordingly offered no evidence against the accused. Basically, they would have asked that the Judge find the defendant not guilty on all of the charges.

The time it takes to get cases to Court is too long, not only for the victims of crime, but also for the accused. Just because you have been accused of a crime, doesn't mean you are guilty, and the whole thing just hangs over the families.

I found a lot of the Ombudsman you are advised to contact, if you are unhappy, to be a complete waste of time. I had dealings with the Information Commissioners Office, PHSO, Solicitors Regulatory Authority, etc. All they seem to do is make sure they have responded to you within a set period of time, and if they haven't, they send a holding letter. Complaints to the Chief Constable normally went unanswered (they still do with the new police chief), the Police and Crime Commissioner is impossible to see, and the only one who went out of his way was my local MP.

Re-writing this has made me remember a lot of things I have previously forgotten, such as the company receiving a letter from one of their accountants saying they had an interested party wanting to buy the firm. When he phoned to find out who it was, it was no surprise that it was my former employers.

Another communication was from a solicitors because I asked for testimonials from a former contact on LinkedIn.

Little things that were sometimes funny, sometimes annoying, often scary, and like having nails hammered into the inside wall of tyres. Having an identical vehicle to his speed up behind me on two or three occasions made me fearful of driving for a time.

No, I cannot attribute it to him, just like the text messages I received from an unknown number. But in civil cases the burden of proof is lower, so on the balance of probability it might be seen as likely, but beyond all reasonable doubt. Even I understand that.

I didn't write this account for revenge, even though he

told the media I was evil. I have told my account because, unless you have a lot of money, you might need to do some of the work yourself. I want to help raise awareness of what stalking can look like and help other victims to deal with it. - the good, the bad and the really ugly. The frustration, the anger and the fear you feel are normal. I don't want anyone to think I'm trying to normalise this crime. I'm most certainly not. More to prepare you for what you may encounter.

I wish I could say that this sorry episode was the last time anything ever happened to me in the workplace, but it isn't. Am I just unlucky?

Maybe.

Is there still a culture in male dominated industries that women should be seen and not heard.

Possibly.

Or is it that greed is in abundance and morals and integrity are not so much.

Whatever is the truth, watch out for my second novel.

EX-PARTE INJUNCTION

ALTHOUGH THIS GOES AGAINST THE TIME LINE, THIS is the most important thing I learned.

It's called an ex-parte injunction.

I spoke to many solicitors who specialise and they wanted £20,000 to represent me. And so, in fear for my life, I represented myself in Court. I paid £280 Court fee and used DAS legal services for advice, well worth the £6 charge for a year. I do not have a legal background or a great education, as previous mentioned. You don't need one either. You need a tiny bit of courage, and any Judge worth their salt, will read your story and give you an injunction if they feel it is justified. You need to allow a day for a Judge to fit you in between trials and in my case, I waited until the end of the day, but I was so relieved when I was finally presented to her. I did not care about the sex of the Judge, but I was happy she was sympathetic.

The Judge asked me just a couple of questions, and from memory they were something like 'Are you really scared that this behaviour will escalate?' and 'why did you feel the need to bring this to the Court?'. Obviously, this great Judge can correct me if I have misquoted her words, but I nearly cried at her warmth and compassion. I shook, and my voice broke, as I explained how scared I was, that as a 'strong woman' myself, the behaviour and action of one person was destroying my life.

This is not 'verbatim' and I do want the court transcripts to be released, so I will apply for them, but the sentiment is honest.

I was awarded my emergency or ex-parte injunction with my education and if you need one, don't care about your spelling, grammar or punctuation, most Judges don't care. I will move on to one who told me off for appearing in-front of him without representation. But he was the exception to 'the rule', and not indicative to the great Judges and Magistrates I have since been before.

In my opinion, it is okay to feel a little daunted, I was, and still am of the legal system. I am no longer intimidated by it. It is well documented that I am highly critical of it. Not the people, who are all trying their hardest in most cases, but please do not let this be a deterrent. If you believe in yourself, you understand your own worth, and you give a care about our society, take yourself out of your comfort zone and voice your opinion. I am marmite to many people. You love me or you loath me.

I have to really care about you to value your opinion of me though.

For the record, the financial controller was acquitted of all charges after 3-years of fighting the system.

The length of time it takes to get matter through the courts isn't just unfair on the 'accusers', it is unfair on the 'accused'. Please do not assume that every 'accuser' is the true victim.

There will be much of this later.

AFFADAVIT

OF

CLAIMANT

V

DEFENDANT

1.  I, ▇▇▇▇▇▇▇▇▇▇, of , ▇▇▇▇▇▇▇, make oath and say as follows:

2.  I make this affidavit based on my personal knowledge, unless otherwise stated, and that the following facts and matters are accurate to the best of my knowledge.

3.  I provide this statement in relation to a series of incidents that I believe will show a course of conduct that my former employer, ▇▇▇▇▇▇▇▇, hereafter known as the Defendant, knowing this would cause me alarm and distress and make me fear for my safety and my life.

4.  I was employed by the Defendants Company, ▇▇▇▇▇▇▇ of ▇▇▇▇▇, ▇▇▇▇▇▇▇▇▇▇▇ from ▇▇▇ until ▇▇. ▇▇▇▇▇ The Defendant is the owner and Chairman of the Business, ▇▇▇▇▇▇▇ ▇▇▇▇▇▇▇▇▇▇▇▇▇▇▇▇▇▇▇▇▇.

5.  At the point of my dismissal, I was employed as a Sales Manager.

6.  I was dismissed for Gross Misconduct, being a breach of trust and a breach of confidence.

7.  Immediately before my dismissal, it became apparent that the Defendant had a junior member of staff access my personal mobile phone account records to see who I was calling and texting.

8.  I met with the Defendant on the ▇▇▇▇▇▇, and he boasted that he had accessed my account 'because he could'.

9.  ▇▇▇▇▇▇▇▇▇▇▇ is an ▇▇▇▇▇▇▇▇▇▇▇▇▇▇▇▇▇▇▇▇▇, and as such has access to their customers call data records for the purpose of completing quarterly reviews and dealing with customers queries.

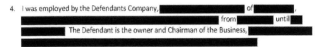

10. I was not a customer of ▇▇▇▇▇▇▇ and complained ▇▇▇ they had allowed this third party visibility to my call data records.

11. On ▇▇▇▇▇▇▇▇ moved my mobile number to a new account number to prevent ▇▇▇▇▇▇▇ from accessing my records.

12. I made a complaint to ███████████ and an investigation followed, and the Defendant was questioned under caution by PC ███████████ of ███████████.

13. The Defendant denied accessing my call data records, the Police have evidence provided under a Court Order from ███████ confirmed the Company had accessed my phone records on 115 separate occasions between ██████ and ██████.

14. The Defendant contacted me by text message and email on the day and the day after he was questioned by the Police, warning me that he would make the true nature of our relationship public.

15. I notified ███████████ and he was warned that he was not to contact me again, or he would be arrested for perverting the course of justice.

16. In ██████ I brought Wrongful and Unfair dismissal claim against ███████████ at ███████████ where the claim was settled on the morning of the hearing with 100% of the schedule of losses paid to me.

17. In ██████, ███████████ dismissed ███████████ for Fraud.

18. The case against the former ███████████ is due to be heard in ██████ and I have information that directly contradicts some of the claims made by individual Board Members that will cast doubt on the credibility of the evidence they have supplied.

19. The file to the breaches of my data are currently with the Prosecuting Authorities who are deciding whether to pursue this matter.

20. In the meantime, I believe the reasons given are the reasons I am being targeted by the Defendant in a course of conduct that could be considered to be harassment.

21. The Police have other evidence that confirms the Defendants private vehicle, ███████████ ██████, ███████████ was in the vicinity of my property on both occasions my cars were painted as referenced in my applications Application for Injunction and CPR Part 8.

22. I have improved the security at my home by updating my house alarm, and my CCTV camera's. I have fitted additional door locks and locks to all downstairs windows. I have internal door locks on every door.

23. The fire department have fitted a lockable flap on my letter box to prevent petrol or other accelerants being put through the letter box. They also gave me advice on risk assessment in the event of a fire at my property and advised me that my house is on a 'watch list' and if they receive a 999 call, three fire appliances, an ambulance and the Police will be despatched.

24. I carry a rape alarm and a spray that covers an attacker with red paint.

25. I am under taking self-defence classes.

26. I have known the defendant for 17-years, 10 years before my employment, during and after.

27. ███████████████████████ nose at a Christmas Party approximately ████
ago, because ███████████████████████████████████.

28. I am aware that a threat was made to the former Financial Controller, and this incident was
reported to ████████████████████. The Defendant has threatened to harm the
████████████, his wife and children after the trial.

29. ███████ is now aware that the Police are waiting to arrest him on his return from holiday
and I fear that I am immediate and serious danger, and would ask the Court to consider this
application.

30. I would ask the Court to consider an Injunction containing a provision to which the power to
arrest is attached.

Signature _____

NAME _____

Date _____


Witness _____

NAME _____

Date _____

**Click here to reset form** | **Click here to print form**

# Application for Injunction
## (General Form)

| Name of court | Claim No. |
|---|---|

Claimant's Name and Ref.

Defendant's Name and Ref.

Fee Account no.

Notes on completion

Tick which boxes apply and specify the legislation where appropriate

(1) Enter the full name of the person making the application

(2) Enter the full name of the person the injunction is to be directed to

(3) Set out any proposed orders requiring acts to be done. Delete if no mandatory order is sought.

(4) Set out here the proposed terms of the injunction order (if the defendant is a limited company delete the wording in brackets and insert 'whether by its servants, agents, officers or otherwise').

(5) Set out here any further terms asked for including provision for costs

(6) Enter the names of all persons who have sworn affidavits or signed statements in support of this application

(7) Enter the names and addresses of all persons upon whom it is intended to serve this application

(8) Enter the full name and address for service and delete as required

☐ By application in pending proceedings

☐ Under Statutory provision _____

☑ This application is made under Part 8 of the Civil Procedure Rules

This application raises issues under the Human Rights Act 1998 ☐ Yes ☐ No

(Seal)

**The Claimant**[1]

**applies to the court for an injunction order in the following terms:**

**The Defendant**[2]

**must**[3]

**The Defendant**

**be forbidden (whether by himself or by instructing or encouraging or permitting any other person)**[4]

From coming within 1 mile of home address of,
or work address of

**And that**[5]

Cost are awarded against the defendant.

**The grounds of this application are set out in the written evidence**

of[6] _____ sworn (signed) on _____

This written evidence is served with this application.

**This application is to be served upon**[7]

**This application is filed by**[8]

(the Solicitors for) the Claimant (Applicant/Petitioner)

whose address for service is

Signed _____ Dated _____

---

This section to be completed by the court

* Name and address of the person application is directed to

To*

of

**This application will be heard by the (District) Judge**

at

on _____ the _____ day of _____ 20 _____ at _____ o'clock

**If you do not attend at the time shown the court may make an injunction order in your absence**

If you do not fully understand this application you should go to a Solicitor, Legal Advice Centre or a Citizens' Advice Bureau

The court office at

is open between 10am and 4pm Mon - Fri. When corresponding with the court, please address all forms and letters to the Court Manager and quote the claim number.

N16A General form of application for injunction (05.14)                    © Crown copyright 2014

**Claim Form (CPR Part 8)**

In the ██████████

Claim no.

Fee Account no.

Claimant

██████████

SEAL

Defendant(s)

██████████

Does your claim include any Issues under the Human Rights Act 1998?  ☐ Yes  ☑ No

**Details of claim** *(see also overleaf)*
THE CLAIMANT SEEKS AND INJUNCTION UNDER THE PREVENTION OF HARASSMENT ACT 1997.

The acts of harassment that support the application are as follows:

a. At ██████████ the claimants car, ██████████ and that of her husband's car, ██████████ were daubed in white gloss paint as they slept. This was reported to the 101 service of the Police and received a crime number of ██████████ The photo's of the damage is attached (A).

b. The Claimant viewed the CCTV footage from three camera's covering the front of her property and identified the offender as ██████████

c. On ██████████ the claimant received a text message from mobile number ██████████ 'Revenge is sweet with patience. Time to strike back. Watch your back lady im coming for you'. The claimant reported this and was given a crime reference number ██████████

Defendant's name and address

██████████

|  | £ |
|---|---|
| Court fee | ██████ |
| Legal representative's costs | |
| Issue date | |

For further details of the courts www.gov.uk/find-court-tribunal.
When corresponding with the Court, please address forms or letters to the Manager and always quote the claim number.

N208 Claim Form (CPR Part 8) (05.14)  © Crown copyright 2014

| Claim no. | |
|---|---|

## Details of claim *(continued)*

d. On ▓▓▓▓ the claimant received a further text message from the same number 'Happy new year lady although for you i dont think its gonna be from the photo i got of you the face looks a disaster already so ill probably leave that alone' This was given a crime reference of ▓▓▓▓

e. On ▓▓▓▓ the claimant received a further text message from the same number 'By the way lady do not even think about going to the old bill you will only make matters worse for yourself and besides you will never know who i am or who i work for'. This was given a crime reference of ▓▓▓▓

f. At ▓▓▓▓ red gloss paint was thrown over the Claimants car. This was given a crime reference of ▓▓▓▓

g. The offender is clearly the same person identified as the original offender and again positively identified as ▓▓▓▓

h. ▓▓▓▓ the claimant received a further text message from the same number 'Im still watching and waiting' This was given a crime reference of ▓▓▓▓

i. On ▓▓▓▓ the file was passed to CID. D C ▓▓▓▓ arranged for the fire service to fit a lockable letter box cover in case the defendant puts a petrol through the letter box, fitted additional fire alarms and provided the Claimant with a rape alarm, and gave general advice on safety and security.

j On ▓▓▓▓ five Police Officers attended the business premises of the Defendant to arrest and search the home and business premises for the phone and SIM card. They were advised he is on holiday and due to return to work on

### Statement of Truth
*(I believe)(The Claimant believes) that the facts stated in these particulars of claim are true.
* I am duly authorised by the claimant to sign this statement.

Full name ▓▓▓▓

Name of claimant's legal representative's firm _____

signed _____   position or office held _____
 *(Claimant)(Litigation friend)        (if signing on behalf of firm or company)
 (Legal representative's solicitor)
                                              *delete as appropriate

Claimant's or claimant's legal representative's address to which documents should be sent if different from overleaf. If you are prepared to accept service by DX, fax or e-mail, please add details.

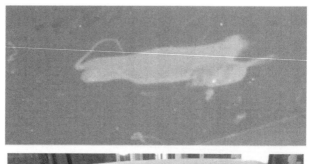

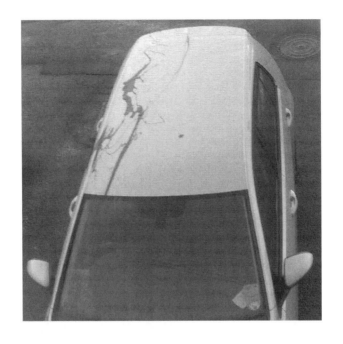

**Injunction Order**

Between ██████████ Defendant

and ██████████ Claimant

██████████

| In the County Court at | |
|---|---|
| | ██████████ |
| **Claim Number** | ██████████ |
| **Claimant** (including ref.) | ██████████ |
| **Defendant** (including ref.) | ██████████ |

**If you do not obey this order you will be guilty of contempt of court and you may be sent to prison**

Before ██████████ sitting at the County Court at ██████████

**UPON HEARING** the Applicant in person

On ██████████ applied to the Court without notice and the court considered an application for an injunction

**The Court ordered that** The Defendant, ██████████

**is forbidden** (whether by himself or by instructing or encouraging or permitting any other person)

1. From coming within 1 mile of home address of ██████████ or work address of ██████████

2. The Defendant shall not harass, intimidate or cause any injury to ██████████

3. There shall be a return date on ██████████ with a time estimate of 1 hour at the County Court at ██████████

4. Costs reserved.

**This order shall remain in force until** 4:00 pm on ██████████ unless before then it is revoked by further order of the court.

*If you do not understand anything in this order you should go to a Solicitor, Legal Advice Centre or a Citizen's Advice Bureau.*

You may be able to get free legal advice. Go online at www.gov.uk/legal-aid for further information.

The court office at the County Court at ██████████ between 10:00 am and 2:00 pm Monday to Friday. When corresponding with the court, please address forms or letters to the Court Manager and quote the claim number. Produced by: ██████

N16(1) General Form of injunction for interlocutory application or originating application
Formal Para - See complete N16 for wording of operating clauses

**Anti-Social Behaviour Injunction Power of Arrest**

| In the County Court at | |
|---|---|
| | ███████████ |
| **Case Number** | ██████████ |
| **Claimant** (including ref.) | ████████████ |
| **Defendant** (including ref.) | ████████████ |

███████████

Before ████████████████████████████████████████████

**UPON HEARING** the Applicant in person

On ██████████ applied to the Court without notice and the court considered an application for an injunction

**The Court ordered that** The Defendant ████████████████████

**is forbidden** (whether by himself or by instructing or encouraging or permitting any other person)

1. From coming within 1 mile of home address of ████████████████████
████████████████████████████████████

2. The Defendant shall not harass, intimidate or cause any injury to ████████████

**Power of Arrest**

And the judge finding:
That the conditions in sections 153A (3) and (4) of the Housing Act 1996 are satisfied,

And the court being satisfied that:
That there is a risk of harm to the person named in section 153A(4)

A power of arrest is attached to this injunction whereby any constable may under the power given in section 155 of the Housing Act 1996, arrest without warrant the defendant if the constable has reasonable cause for the suspecting the defendant is in breach of this injunction.

**This power of arrest was ordered on** ████████████████████

**Defendant**

███████████████

**Note to Arresting Officer**

Where the defendant is arrested under the power given by section 155 of the Housing Act 1996, that section requires that:
- the defendant shall be brought before the judge within the period of 24 hours begining at the time of his arrest;
- the defendant shall not be released within that period except on the direction of the judge;

The court office at the County Court at ████████████████ is open between 10:00 am and 2:00 pm Monday to Friday. When corresponding with the court, please address forms or letters to the Court Manager and quote the claim number ████████████

**Notice of Injunction hearing**

| In the County Court at | ████████ |
|---|---|

| Claim Number | ████████ |
|---|---|
| Date | ████████ |

| ████████ | 1ˢᵗ Claimant Ref |
|---|---|
| ████████ | 1ˢᵗ Defendant Ref |

TAKE NOTICE that the Injunction hearing will take place on

████████

at the County Court at ████████

When you should attend

1 hour has been allowed for the Injunction hearing

**Please Note:** This case may be released to another Judge, possibly at a different Court

**IF YOU ARE SUBMITTING DOCUMENTS IN RESPECT OF A HEARING PLEASE ENSURE THAT THE CASE NUMBER AND HEARING DATE CLEARLY ENDORSED SO THAT YOUR CORRESPONDENCE CAN BE ATTACHED TO THE FILE IN TIME FOR THE HEARING.**

Cases are listed in accordance with local hearing arrangements determined by the Judiciary and implemented by Court Staff. Every effort is made to ensure that hearings start either at the time specified or as soon as possible thereafter. However listing practices or other factors may mean that delay is unavoidable.

Furthermore in some instances a case may be released to another Judge possibly at a different Court. Please contact the Court for further information on the listing arrangements that may apply to your hearing.

For general on line queries and information this Court Office can be contacted at enquiries@████████

If you need legal advice or assistance you should contact Civil Legal Advice on 0845 345 4345 or visit their website at www.gov.uk/legal-aid

If you are unable to attend the hearing, you can apply for an adjournment but there is an application fee of £50.00 to do so. However, no fee is payable to adjourn a hearing at least 14 days before the date of the hearing, with the consent of the other side.

The court office at the County Court at ████████ is open between 10:00 am and 2:00 pm Monday to Friday. When corresponding with the court, please address forms or letters to the Court Manager and quote the claim number. ████████

N24 Notice of PTR/Adjnd/Restored/Hrg/Management Conference

## [ 3 ]

PAPERS SERVED

I HAD PAPERS SERVED ON THE DEFENDANT ON Sunday 15<sup>th</sup> March 2015.

I telephoned his home phone with my number withheld to confirm he had returned from his holiday. Once I established he was at home, a Private Detective served the papers. I was eating lunch when I received the call to say he had 'been served', but instead of relief, there was a feeling of mixed emotion.

Would this 'trigger' an event? Would this bring him to his senses?

He contacted the Investigating Detective Constable and was interviewed under caution on Tuesday 17<sup>th</sup> March 2015. He co-operated for a time.

His defence and argument seemed credible, I think, for a while. He made several allegations against me, and thought he had done enough to tarnish my reputation. That is until he was asked why his vehicle was captured on ANPR camera's a mile away from our house, approximately 13-minutes before my company vehicle was vandalised on each occasion.

He then turned the interview into a 'No Comment' interview from there on in. He then provided the police with bank statements to 'prove' that he had not purchased paint around the time. I questioned the allegations with the investigating officer, and provided proof that the allegations were false without prompting or a request made.

Reading a defence, when you know it is predominantly lies, is frustrating and made me livid. I believe this is usual, but I have learned that this is a waste of emotion. Rather than cry, get angry, hate the world, I set out to prove to the Court he was an absolute liar, and that I could evidence everything that I stated.

By this time, he had employed the services of a firm of solicitors in Leicester for the Tribunal, and they dipped in and out of other parts of this story. They don't come out of it too well in my opinion, but that will be for you to decide. He used a criminal solicitor when he was interviewed by the Police and during the trial. And then he used another firm for the Injunction and Undertaking Civil case.

I always acknowledged that everyone in this country is entitled to a defence, but when you are acting for yourself through necessity against a millionaire who doesn't like to lose, the 'system' can feel a little unbalanced. I met with one of his representatives at an event recently, and we had an interesting exchange. The representative seemed a little wary, even cautious when I introduced myself, and seemed embarrassed, even apologetic by the various exchanges, where we locked horns.

I have long since forgiven them for their part in the story, but did smile to myself when I was advised that they were only acting on the clients instructions, even though the evidence pointed to a guilty verdict.

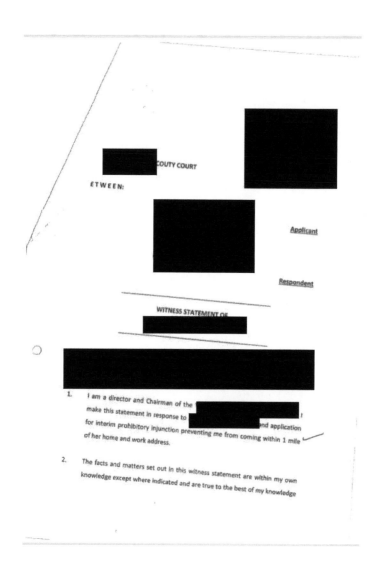

COUTY COURT

ETWEEN:

Applicant

Respondent

WITNESS STATEMENT OF

1. I am a director and Chairman of the make this statement in response to for interim prohibitory injunction preventing me from coming within 1 mile of her home and work address.

2. The facts and matters set out in this witness statement are within my own knowledge except where indicated and are true to the best of my knowledge

and belief. Where reference is made to facts which are outside my own knowledge, I set out the source of my information and I believe such information to be true.

3. There is now produced and shown to me a bundle of documents marked CS1 to which reference will be made in the course of this statement in the form [CS1.page].

## Background

4. As stated above, ███████████████████████████████████████████████████████████████████████████████████████████████████

5. I can confirm to the Court I have known the Applicant for ████████████ years. Most recently she worked for ███████████████████ until her dismissal for gross misconduct in ████████

6. ██████████████████████████ referred to at paragraphs 17 and 18 of the Applicant's statement was arrested by the Police on suspicion of fraud in the spring of ██ It was discovered funds to the tune of ████████ were missing from ████████████████████

7. In the period after his arrest, all members of staff including the Applicant were told not to communicate with ████████ as to do so may jeopardise an ongoing Police investigation and would be treated as a serious incident by the Company. In the autumn of ████ it was discovered that the Claimant had been in contact with ████████ and a disciplinary investigation was started against the Applicant.

8.  The disciplinary action was conducted by the ███████████ at the time ███████████ and the applicant was dismissed as a result of this investigation in ███████ ███████████████████████

9.  ███████ following the Police's investigation has now been charged with 4 counts of obtaining money by deception and his matter is listed at ███████ ███████████████████████ and other directors are due to give evidence during this Trial and I understand the Applicant is going to give evidence for the Defence.

### Unauthorised Access of the Applicants Mobile Phone Records

10. ███████████████████████ We offer business ███████████ companies and individuals alike. The Applicant began her business contract with ███████ ███████████████████████ As part of our ███████████████████████ is entitled to a share of the mobile phone bill at the end of each month and this data is sent to us by ███████ that we can verify what amounts are due to us and also to analyze the data for future sales.

11. The Claimant terminated her most recent contract with ███████████ which would otherwise have run until ███████████ I enclose an extract showing ███████████ share report which also shows the dates the Applicant held her contract with ███████████ as well as the bill amounts (CS1-2).

12. At paragraph 7 I refute the allegation that I had a junior member of the Company access the Applicant's records. I had no reason for doing so

personally. An employee of ███████████ have accessed her records as part of the Company's affairs and the Applicant would have been aware of this having held the post of ████████ She confirms this at paragraph 9 of her Affidavit.

13. In respect of the Applicant's allegation she was not a client of ████████ this will easily be disproved on disclosure from the Applicant herself or ████████████ In any event, ███████ were passed information regarding the Applicant's spending patterns ███████ nd had no ways of obtaining this data themselves. The Applicant fails to mention she has already made failed complaints regarding this matter to ███████████████████████ ███████

14. I can confirm to the Court I was questioned by the Police regarding this matter and I also confirm this was a voluntary interview and I have not heard since from the Police regarding this.

## Allegations of Harassment

15. I received papers regarding this injunction application on ███████████ I can confirm I received no enclosures to the Claim form or Affidavit therefore I have not been able to see the photographs the Applicant refers to.

16. In response to the Applicants allegations I attended a voluntary interview under caution at ████████████████████████████ enclose the Police's notice regarding the recording of my interview which shows this was a voluntary interview contrary to the Applicants assertions at paragraph 29 of her Affidavit (CS3-4). I also enclose a copy of my written statement which I handed to the Police at this interview (CS5).

17. During the course of this interview I was shown the CCTV footage the Applicant refers to in her Claim form. I invite the Court to view this footage and compare the same to paragraph b of the Applicants Claim form. It is impossible to identify who the individual is in these images.

18. Paragraphs c, d, e and g of the Claim form allege someone contacted the Applicant by ▮▮▮ telephone. The Applicant fails to directly allege this number belongs to me and I am not sure how these contacts are relevant to this matter. Assuming it will be alleged that these contacts are attributed to me, I refute this completely.

19. I have no reason for making the threats as alleged by the Applicant and I fear this is a more sinister attempt to interfere with existing Court proceedings in respect of ▮▮▮▮ prosecution. As stated above, I and other ▮▮▮▮ ▮▮▮▮ are due to give evidence on behalf of the Crown and I understand the Applicant is giving evidence on behalf of the Defence.

20. If as the Applicant alleges at paragraph 18 she has evidence which will undermine the Crowns case against ▮▮▮▮ it is astonishing the same has not been disclosed to the Police and CPS. It is absurd for the Applicant to suggest that because of this evidence somehow I am targeting her even though she does not say so directly.

21. As stated in my written statement to the Police on the current evidence before the Police and this Court, it is equally conceivable the Applicant sent those messages to herself to try and obtain this injunction so that my credibility is compromised as witness for the Crown at the upcoming Trial. Whilst I have no evidence for my assertion as is the case with the Claimant's own assertions, ▮▮▮▮▮▮▮▮▮▮ supplies ▮▮▮ ▮▮▮▮▮ contract whilst I understand the Applicant works for ▮▮▮ ▮▮▮▮▮ which does supply sim cards among other things.

## Other relevant matters

22.    I can confirm to the Court I have never been arrested by the Police for any crime and the only record I have with them relates to speeding fines and other traffic offences.

23.    The fact the Police have not arrested me regarding the numerous allegations by the Applicant and that I am not subject to Police Bail or otherwise is entirely contrary to the picture the Applicant has painted of me in her statement. It is also evident the Applicant has failed to give a full account of all facts and matters relevant to her allegations for example her failed complainants to ███████████████████ the relevance of ongoing Court proceedings in respect of ██████ and her false allegations regarding my arrest.

## Conclusion

24.    I would request the Court to quash the current interim injunction as it is without basis and has no evidence to support it. It is particularly concerning that the affidavit contains matters that go back to ███ and some that are even older which are then linked with more recent occurrences which then somehow come together to form the basis for this injunction some 6 weeks before the prosecution of a former employee.

25.    If this matter is not disposed of entirely at the hearing on ████████ I would request the Court that Trial is expedited in this matter so that it is dealt with before Trial in ██████ case.

**STATEMENT OF TRUTH**

I believe that the facts set out in this Witness Statement are true.

Date:

| Period_Date | Account_No | MPN | Contract_Start_Date | Contract_End_Date | Expr1 |
|---|---|---|---|---|---|
| 01/12/2009 | 4729█ | ███771 | 15/12/2009 | 15/12/2012 | 29.41 |
| 01/01/2010 | 4729█ | ███771 | 15/12/2009 | 15/12/2012 | 87.57 |
| 01/02/2010 | 4729█ | ███771 | 15/12/2009 | 15/12/2012 | 35.48 |
| 01/03/2010 | 4729█ | ███771 | 15/12/2009 | 15/12/2012 | 36.31 |
| 01/04/2010 | 4729█ | ███771 | 15/12/2009 | 15/12/2012 | 34.39 |
| 01/05/2010 | 4729█ | ███771 | 15/12/2009 | 15/12/2012 | 44.18 |
| 01/06/2010 | 4729█ | ███771 | 15/12/2009 | 15/12/2012 | 42.84 |
| 01/07/2010 | 4729█ | ███771 | 15/12/2009 | 15/12/2012 | 131.12 |
| 01/08/2010 | 4729█ | ███771 | 15/12/2009 | 15/12/2012 | 35.66 |
| 01/09/2010 | 4729█ | ███771 | 15/12/2009 | 15/12/2012 | 34.39 |
| 01/10/2010 | 4729█ | ███771 | 15/12/2009 | 15/12/2012 | 35.92 |
| 01/11/2010 | 4729█ | ███771 | 15/12/2009 | 15/12/2012 | 36.82 |
| 01/12/2010 | 4729█ | ███771 | 15/12/2009 | 15/12/2012 | 41.22 |
| 01/01/2011 | 4729█ | ███771 | 15/12/2009 | 15/12/2012 | 35.85 |
| 01/02/2011 | 4729█ | ███771 | 15/12/2009 | 15/12/2012 | 34.86 |
| 01/03/2011 | 4729█ | ███771 | 15/12/2009 | 15/12/2013 | 35.76 |
| 01/04/2011 | 4729█ | ███771 | 15/12/2009 | 15/12/2012 | 35.57 |
| 01/05/2011 | 4729█ | ███771 | 15/12/2009 | 15/12/2012 | 46.07 |
| 01/06/2011 | 4729█ | ███771 | 15/12/2009 | 15/12/2012 | 34.47 |
| 01/07/2011 | 4729█ | ███771 | 15/12/2009 | 15/12/2012 | 55.2 |
| 01/08/2011 | 4729█ | ███771 | 15/12/2009 | 15/12/2012 | 35.42 |
| 01/09/2011 | 4729█ | ███771 | 15/12/2009 | 15/12/2012 | 34.52 |
| 01/10/2011 | 4729█ | ███771 | 15/12/2009 | 15/12/2012 | 39.33 |
| 01/11/2011 | 4729█ | ███771 | 15/12/2009 | 15/12/2012 | 44.19 |
| 01/12/2011 | 4729█ | ███771 | 15/12/2009 | 15/12/2012 | 38.13 |
| 01/01/2012 | 4729█ | ███771 | 15/12/2009 | 15/12/2012 | 82.38 |
| 01/02/2012 | 4729█ | ███771 | 15/12/2009 | 15/12/2012 | 34.44 |
| 01/03/2012 | 4729█ | ███771 | 15/12/2009 | 15/12/2012 | 35.45 |
| 01/04/2012 | 4729█ | ███771 | 15/12/2009 | 15/12/2012 | 34.39 |
| 01/05/2012 | 4729█ | ███771 | 15/12/2009 | 15/12/2012 | 36.35 |
| 01/06/2012 | 4729█ | ███771 | 15/12/2009 | 15/12/2012 | 34.7 |
| 01/07/2012 | 4729█ | ███771 | 15/12/2009 | 15/12/2012 | 41.8 |
| 01/08/2012 | 4729█ | ███771 | 15/12/2009 | 15/12/2012 | 34.62 |
| 01/09/2012 | 4729█ | ███771 | 15/12/2009 | 15/12/2012 | 35.02 |
| 01/10/2012 | 4729█ | ███771 | 15/12/2009 | 15/12/2012 | 42.5095 |
| 01/11/2012 | 4729█ | ███771 | 15/12/2009 | 15/12/2012 | 65.63 |
| 01/12/2012 | 4729█ | ███771 | 15/12/2009 | 15/12/2012 | 36.13 |
| 01/01/2013 | 47296█ | ███771 | 12/01/2013 | 12/01/2015 | 37.97 |
| 01/02/2013 | 47296█ | ███771 | 12/01/2013 | 12/01/2015 | 52.56 |
| 01/03/2013 | 47296█ | ███771 | 12/01/2013 | 12/01/2015 | 155.76 |
| 01/04/2013 | 47296█ | ███771 | 12/01/2013 | 12/01/2015 | 37.15 |
| 01/05/2013 | 47296█ | ███771 | 12/01/2013 | 12/01/2015 | 40.34 |
| 01/06/2013 | 47296█ | ███771 | 12/01/2013 | 12/01/2015 | 48.69 |
| 01/07/2013 | 47296█ | ███771 | 12/01/2013 | 12/01/2015 | 44.93 |
| 01/08/2013 | 47296█ | ███771 | 12/01/2013 | 12/01/2015 | 41.1 |
| 01/09/2013 | 47296█ | ███771 | 12/01/2013 | 12/01/2015 | 38.83 |
| 01/10/2013 | 47296█ | ███771 | 12/01/2013 | 12/01/2015 | 55.21 |
| 01/11/2013 | 47296█ | ███771 | 12/01/2013 | 12/01/2015 | 63.63 |
| 01/12/2013 | 47296█ | ███771 | 12/01/2013 | 12/01/2015 | 39.37 |

1

| | | | | | |
|---|---|---|---|---|---|
| 01/01/2014 | 527 | 771 | 12/01/2013 | 12/01/2015 | 55.84 |
| 01/02/2014 | 527 | 771 | 12/01/2013 | 12/01/2015 | 36.92 |
| 01/03/2014 | 527 | 771 | 12/01/2013 | 12/01/2015 | 41.44 |
| 01/04/2014 | 527 | 771 | 12/01/2013 | 12/01/2015 | 45.02 |
| 01/05/2014 | 527 | 771 | 12/01/2013 | 12/01/2015 | 41.79 |
| 01/06/2014 | 527 | 771 | 12/01/2013 | 12/01/2015 | 50.14 |
| 01/07/2014 | 527 | 771 | 12/01/2013 | 12/01/2015 | 358.16 |

## [ 4 ]

RETURN TO COURT

PLEASE BEAR IN MIND, I WAS UNSURE AT THIS STAGE what was expected of me when we returned to court.

I was supported by a friend who was allowed to sit in the public gallery, while he was represented at the table with a small legal team.

I was daunted, to say the least, but I soon relaxed when Recorder Richard Smith started to ask his team relevant questions, and although I didn't follow everything that was going on, I did ask a question between the difference between an injunction and an undertaking, and His Honour very kindly explained that both had a power of arrest if the terms were broken, but one was given, the other was 'volunteered, and it was suggested by His Honour that if the defendant did not volunteer an undertaking, he would allow a further injunction.

Recorder Smith was one of the kindest people I met during this experience, and I absolutely 'loved' him on this day, and unknown to me at the time, at another trial sometime later, where I was a defence witness involving the former financial controller.

My friend and I promptly left the court, and as we returned to our car, we did laugh as the defendant had been given a parking ticket.

Anyway, I think what I am trying to say is I don't know if the following was entirely necessary. I was never told I had to prepare a rebuttal to his defence, but I felt I needed to be prepared, just in case.

IN THE ███████ COUNTY COURT

BETWEEN:

███████

<u>Applicant</u>

And

███████

<u>Respondent</u>

---

WITNESS STATEMENT OF

███████

---

I, ███████ do hereby make this statement in relation to the incidents of harassment referred to in my affidavit of Friday ███████ and the Respondents statement of ███████

I have no criminal record, not even a traffic offence.

<u>Background</u>

1. ███████ he former Financial Controller of ███████ was dismissed and arrested in ███████ On the day of his dismissal, I asked the Board of Directors if we were going to sue ███████ who had prepared our last set of Accounts, and ███████ and another firm of accountants who had audited the Accounts as part of the due diligence for the acquisition of ███████ I was instructed by the Managing Director to shut up.

2. Staff were advised that ███████ had falsified sick notes and that he had not suffered a stroke as we had all believed.

3. When I was dismissed from ███████ emailed my intention to Appeal against the decision, and requested information under a Subject Access Request to be supplied to me by the Company in order for me to prepare the Appeal. See email trail starting with my email ███████ (See exhibit 1)

4. The Respondent responded to the email on ███████████ stating that he was happy to meet with me on a 'Without Prejudice' basis and that there was no need to have an aide present.

5. I replied on ███████████ and we agreed to meet at the Starbucks in ███████████ ███████████ for what I believed to be an 'off the record' chat.

6. At that meeting, the Respondent asked me what hold ███████████ He said my email to him 'smacked of ████ He asked why I had contacted ███████████ I had been dismissed. I said to the Respondent that I was aware the ████ had received bonuses from the business and the Respondent replied that he had not. He said the Police would want to take a statement from me and he would contact them immediately. It became clear that ████ ███████████ had accessed my personal mobile phone account.

7. No resolution was agreed.

8. On the ███████████ I received some of the information I requested by Recorded Delivery together with the Respondents letter dated ███████████ (see Exhibit 2).

9. Again, I emailed the Respondent on ███████████ where I stated I believe I was dismissed in an attempt to avoid paying guaranteed bonuses that were due to be paid in ███████████ Bonuses the Respondent is now claiming he had no knowledge off. (See Exhibit 3).

10. I received a further email from ███████████ ███████████ inviting me to meet with the Respondent. (see exhibit 4)

11. We met at ███████████ and I was offered a Settlement Agreement. However by the middle of December, my solicitor still had not seen sight of the Settlement Agreement, and I instructed him to proceed to Tribunal. When we did receive the Settlement Agreement, there were several clauses that were unpalatable, and I refused to sign it on that basis.

12. Again, I requested information under a Subject Access Request. This request was ignored.

13. I chased the Respondent again on the ███████████ stating that the information was now 5 days overdue of the 40 days recommended by the Information Commissioners Office and asked for the information be furnished to me by the ███████████

14. I received a response on the ███████████ that the Respondent did not see the relevance of my request and he refused to supply the information.

15. I responded that it wasn't for him to decide the relevance, and that I had every right to the information requested.

16. Again, on the ███████████ the Respondent responded that 'I can decide what I want.'

17. During ███████████ I requested my Port Authorisation Code without termination charges from ███ the basis that my call data records were being viewed by ████████ ███████████

18. The request was denied. I was advised that they were a 'trusted partner'.

19. I had a long telephone conversation with ███████████████████ and confirmed my allegations against the Company in an email on the same day. (See exhibit 5).

20. My mobile number was moved to a new account number on ███████████ in an attempt to stop ████████████████████ visibility to my account on line. (see exhibit 6)

21. I was dismissed from the business by the ███████████████ who was subsequently dismissed himself in ███████████████ took action against ████████ Communications when they tried to tell him he was not employed by the Company and that he was only ever a Consultant.

22. I believe that claim was settled to ███████████

23. ███████████████████████████████████ charges Fraud by False Representation and not the Respondents claim of obtaining money by deception. 6 other allegations were not pursued, such as falsifying doctor's sick notes when he had a stroke.

24. I have seen the charges against ███████████ do have information that directly contradicts some of the points raised in the statements of the Board of Directors.

25. ███████████████████████████ dismissal will be heard if he is acquitted of the charges against him.

26. ███████████████ has advised staff members that ████████ has been charged with ██████████

Unauthorised Access of the Mobile Phone Records

27. As I have already stated, ███████████████████ full visibility to the call data records of their customers for the purpose of review. The web portal gives a warning when you log on to the account that if you are not authorised to access the account, you are breaching the Computer Misuse Act. (see exhibit 7)

28. I had been a ███████████████████████████ ███████████████████ and as such my call data records should have been removed from the web portal ██████████

29. I have supplied my signed Contract (exhibit 8)

30. I have supplied the receipt from ████████ confirming the date and my mobile number and the IMEI (serial number) of the handset supplied (see exhibit 9)

31. I have supplied a IMEI enquiry supplied by ████████████████████ and was supply for sale on ████████ (see exhibit 10)

32. I supply also a copy of an ████████████████ to confirm the phone was in my personal name at my home address and was not a company supplied mobile number. (see exhibit 11)

33. I met with ████████████ to give a statement in relation to the allegations against ████████ and I emailed her in ████████ stating that I wished to make an official complaint against ████████

34. I have been given access to the Police Investigation File by ████████████ I have included this (see exhibit 13), but I have numbered pages 1 to 38.

35. During his interview with PC ████████████████ the Respondent repeatedly denied accessing or having any knowledge that my account was accessed by anyone in the business (see page 19 and 20 of exhibit 13).

36. Page 23 of the bundle shows a Statement by DC ████████████ who confirms that ████████████████████████████████████ handed DC ████████ a dictaphone which had a recording of the meeting between the respondent and myself on the ████████████ DC ████████ has also confirmed this in an email to me. (see exhibit 22)

37. On the same recording was a meeting between the Respondent and an un-named female.

38. The transcript of this meeting is shown at Page 37 and 38 of the bundle. In this transcript, highlighted the Respondent says to the female 'She says well the only way you could know that is if you got access to my call records and then we are talking on a very different level now. I say all I'm saying is I know you have been in communication with him, so I didn't say I had got access to call records, although I did have them with me as well but I didn't use them obviously'.

39. The Respondent has stated in his section 10 that ████████████████ is entitled to a share of a customer's bill at the end of each month and this data is sent to us ████ to verify what amounts are due to them and also to analyse the data for future sales.

40. This is rather misleading. ████████ Revenue Share Report to the company each month, with shows the clients bill total, and the percentage of Revenue due to ████████

████████ There is no requirement of the Company to access the customer's bills online to confirm the amount. During my employment, there was never an incident of ██ falsifying the Revenue Share Report, only that they paid us for numbers that we were not entitled to. Too my knowledge, this was never reported ████ but the Respondents own statement clearly shows the company received Revenue from my number after I upgraded directly ███████████.

41. With approximately 42,000 mobile phone numbers on the base and over 3,500 customers, accessing each customers Call Data Records to confirm the bill amount would take staff members hundreds of hours.

42. The Court Order that ████████████ secured to obtain the evidence that my personal mobile phone account had been accessed confirms that ██████████████████ did not merely look at the bill amount to ensure the revenue had been paid correctly. It also shows that the Call Data Records had been accessed to see who I was calling and texting.

43. To my knowledge ████████████████████ till hold these records, and they potentially have over ██████████████████ and texts that they are not entitled to.

44. I was unaware that █████████████████ received ██ of my mobile phone bill after i upgraded with the ███████████████ but as I had made them aware that I upgraded directly, and they still received revenue, I believe they are guilty of obtaining money by deception themselves in not advising ██████████.

45. ██████████████████ did not supply me with any equipment when I upgraded, and therefore knew I was not a customer.

46. PC ███████████████████████████████ to provide a copy of the Contract, receipt and delivery note from ████████████ MEI (serial number) was supplied to the Company.

47. This was never supplied because it did not exist.

48. The ICO have confirmed that the account has been accessed on 115 separate occasions before and after I left the business, from ████████████████████████ with the Police report confirming ███████████████████████████████████████ person who accessed my account. ██████ has not been questioned by the Police as he moved to ████████████.

49. The Respondent did send me a text message on the day he was to be questioned by the Police at ████████████████████ that said "██████ am being interviewed by the police, (voluntarily), re data protection issues, which I don't have an issue with as we are fully complaint and have not broken any rules, certainly the ICO are satisfied, however

questions will be raised as to our relationship and past history, so it might be prudent for you to pre warn ▮ before this gets into the public domain. ▮▮▮

50. I then received an email at ▮▮▮▮▮▮ that reads ▮▮▮ just to let you know that I was interviewed by the Police today re data protection issues which wasn't a problem. They will be talking to me again but more in depth and questions will be asked about the personal relationship between you and me and our history, so you might want to discuss this with ▮ rather than him find out when it hits the public domain. ▮▮▮▮▮▮

51. I received an identical email the following day to my work email address, but I no longer have a copy.

52. All correspondence were sent to PC ▮▮▮ and he advised me that he had spoken to the Respondent and his solicitors ▮▮▮ to advise them that he was not to have contact with me and if he did, he could be arrested for perverting the course of justice.

53. The ICO have confirmed that it is unlikely that ▮▮▮ has complied with the requirements of the Data Protection Act. This is because the incorrect Revenue code was applied to my ▮▮▮▮▮ having access to the billing records of my account. (see exhibit 16).

54. I requested information from the ICO in a Freedom of Information request and the ICO have confirmed that the DC Action Required. This means the ▮▮▮▮▮ had been ordered or requested to action a request made by the ICO.

55. In respect of the Respondents assertions in section 13, I have received an email from an ▮▮▮▮▮ who has confirmed that ▮▮▮▮▮ channel is aware of the situation and advised that it is being dealt with within the appropriate department within ▮ (see exhibit 18).

56. ▮ aware of the many serious misdemeanours of the Company, such as staff signing customers into ▮▮▮ without their knowledge or consent, and ▮▮▮ have had to reverse the Contracts for a number of customers on the instruction of ▮ when they have been unable to produce a signed Contract. I have been involved with several of the reversals. I have been advised ▮ are losing patience with ▮▮▮▮▮

57. I am aware that ▮▮▮▮▮ which means they buy wholesale minutes on the ▮▮▮▮▮ and rebill this as ▮▮▮ There is a suggestion that they have done this after 25years of being loyal to ▮▮▮▮▮ to decide to terminate their Contract.

58. I can confirm I did not receive 115 tariff reviews from ███████████████ between
████████████████████

Allegations of Harassment

59. The Respondent did contact DC ████████████████████ and
volunteered to answer questions. However DC ████████ will of course be able to confirm
my assertion that five Police Officers attended the offices of ████████████
███████████████████████████████████████ and was advised that
the Respondent was ████████████████████ Which is the reason this application
was made before he returned ████████████ I suspect he would have been advised that the
Police had attended the office and he would be angry.

60. In the Respondents statement he informed DC ████████ that I could be sending myself text
messages to discredit himself in an attempt to 'get ████████ off the charges, and I am
trying to set the Respondent up. He alleges I have received bonus payments that he knew
nothing about.

61. Although I have not been asked to, I have provided DC ████████ with payslips showing
bonus payments together with emails where the Respondent was copied in that mention
future bonuses.

62. I have also provided messages to my former line manager ████████████ who was
employed as the ████████████████████ and to ████████████
████████ that all mention my bonuses.

63. I refer again to Exhibit 3 where I stated I was dismissed in a blatant attempt not to pay
bonuses due in ███████████████████████ These bonuses totalled circ
£24,000. See exhibit 19.

64. Although the Respondent has described the circumstances surrounding my dismissal, he has
not mentioned the subsequent Tribunal which was listed for two days at ████████
Employment Tribunal.

65. I was offered a Settlement Agreement by ████████████ hat again requested that I withdraw
actions with the ICO, and agree to a nine month restrictive covenant. It was suggested that I
withdraw the complaint to ████████████ I refused to sign such an agreement and
was happy to go ahead with the Tribunal. In the end, I was offered a far more agreeable
offer which was agreed before lunch time on the first day.

66. I have also provided the Settlement agreement for the Court to view, as the Respondent has
failed to mention in his statement that we did settle on the morning of the Tribunal for
£33,500 which has been paid. (see exhibit 20).

67. If I had received bonus payments that I was not entitled to, I would have expected ███████ ███████████ o notify the Police with allegations against me or indeed ██████ f we have colluded in some way. I have only been questioned once by DC ██████ nd this was at the request of ██████████ ot the Respondent as indicated in our meeting on █ ██████████

68. The Tribunal was 9-months after my dismissal and if I had received bonus payments I was not entitled to, or the Respondent was not aware of, as he suggests, he would not have paid me a penny unless ordered by the Court, and he certainly would not have offered figures ranging from £15,000 to the £33,500 we settled on.

69. It is offensive and a blatant lie to suggest he did not know I received bonuses as both he, ██████████████████████ and myself had extensive meetings agreeing the bonus structure that applied to both myself and ████████████ and covered a three year period. If as he claims, he had no knowledge of my bonus, I would seriously question his suitability to hold the position of █████████████████

70. I was employed by ████████████████████ when I had CCTV installed at my property and the Respondent was well aware that I had cameras on the front and back of my house. I don't think I ever mentioned I had the side of the property covered too.

71. Although the offender is wearing a half face balaclava and a cap and what looks like golf waterproofs on, in an attempt to hide his identity, I can still identify this as the Respondent, as have others who have seen the footage. I also have a photograph of the Respondent wearing a balaclava when he climbed ████████████████████████████

72. These photographs, amongst others have been sent to a Facial Mapping Expert, together with the CCTV footage, from both my house and the Supermarket next door. They have requested additional information from me, and once I am able to provide this, they will be able to make a comparison for the Court.

73. The respondent has also failed to mention in his statement that the last 25 minutes of the interview he offered no comment, particularly when DC ████████ questioned why his vehicle was caught on the BOF cameras (with number plate recognition) on both the ██████ ████████████████████████ heading in the direction of my house 7 minutes before each offence was committed. The Respondent offered no explanation whatsoever.

74. The respondent has given DC ██████ permission to access his bank account records and the Police hope to find purchases from a DIY shop on either or both dates and the purchase of a SIM card or mobile phone. Realistically, they may not if the paint was laying around in the garage or he paid cash for any purchase.

75. DC ████ will be on duty at ████████████████████ and will be happy to confirm to the Court that the statements I have made regarding the Respondents interview are correct and as described by DC ████████████████████

76. On the balance of probability, I think it is likely that the text messages were sent by the Respondent although they were not sent from the mobile phone number I know he uses. However ████████ re assisting the Police with their enquiries.

77. Again, on the balance of probability, as the Respondent has failed to answer the question of why his ████████████ was caught on camera at approximately ████████████ ████████████████████████████████ believe the Injunction Order of ████████ should be upheld and made permanent.

78. The Respondent might like to explain to the Court why his ████████ was caught on camera travelling from the direction of ████████████████████ now he has had a week to prepare his answer.

79. The suggestion that I have fabricated this sustained period of harassment is as ludicrous as it is offensive. On two of the occasions I have received text messages I have been at work with others who witnessed my receipt and response. On one occasion I was at home with my husband.

80. I do have another mobile phone that I carry that has 999 on a speed dial in case I am attacked. I am happy to disclose this number to the Court to confirm it is not the same number that has sent me the threatening messages.

81. I have co-operated with the Police, with DC ████████████████████ and most recently with PC ████████████████████ whenever asked to.

82. The Respondents allegations that I received bonuses that he was unaware of is simply a lie, and I question whether the Respondent has perjured himself in this Court.

83. With regard to section 24 of the Respondents statement that it is concerning that my affidavit relates to occurrences from ████████████ before the trial. The relevance of the company accessing my call data records ██████ re relevant as this was a form of harassment.

84. I did not influence the timing of the criminal damage or the text messages. In fact, I think the Respondent himself was responsible for the timing, knowing I had to give a statement to solicitors, ████████████████████

85. I categorically deny colluding with ████████ in an attempt to somehow get ████ out of his trial.

86. I stated to DC ██████████████████ when I gave my statement in ████████
██████ and I maintain, that I do not know if ████████ is guilty or not, and believe only the
Jury have the right to make that decision based on the facts presented.

87. However, the Respondent has made the same allegation against me receiving bonuses that I
was not entitled to as he made against ████████ The Respondent has not made an
official complaint to the Police at the time of this statement, and I have been in contact with
DC ██████████████████████████████ during Friday and the
weekend.

88. The Respondent did pay ████████ bonuses that he claims he has no knowledge off in
██████████████████████ after both myself and ████████ had left the
Company. Perhaps the Respondent can explain why he authorised these payments but 18-
months after I left the company and 9 months after the company paid me £33,500 as a
result of the Tribunal, he suddenly claims he has no knowledge of the bonuses.

89. If a complaint is made in the future, I will rely on evidence from this statement to form part
of my defence.

90. I believe that the Respondent has broken the terms of the Settlement Agreement in the
course of conduct that can be seen to be harassment.

91. The Respondent has no legitimate reason to have to be within one mile of my house or my
place of work, or indeed myself or my husband.  He does not have family living in the area,
and as he states himself, he has 70 staff to visit any business clients in the area.

<u>STATEMENT OF TRUTH</u>

I believe that the facts set out in this Witness Statement are true.

Signed

Name
Dated

IN THE ████████ COUNTY COURT

BETWEEN:

████████████████

<u>Applicant</u>

And

████████████████

<u>Respondent</u>

WITNESS STATEMENT OF

████████████

████████████

I, ████████████████████████████████ do hereby make this statement in relation to the incidents of harassment referred to in my affidavit of ████████ ████████ and the Respondents statement of ████████ ████████████████████████

<u>**Unauthorised Access of the Applicants Mobile Phone Records**</u>

1. In ████████ statement of the ████████ ████████ provided a copy of a Revenue Share Report, which showed ████████████████████████████████ on my mobile phone account until I ported to ████████ ████████

2. As I had previously been told ████████ my mobile number had been moved to a new account to prevent such access, I was unaware until reading the statement that ████████ continued to receive Revenue on my number.

3. I contacted ████████████████████████████ had accessed my account at any point during ████████████████

4. ████ confirmed that ████████████████████ accessed my account in ████████, and would ask ████████ to explain the reason why. (see exhibit 2)

5. ███████████████ have now stated to ██ that they accessed my account in ████ ███ at my request, having returned from holiday, and concerned about the bill, I requested a member of staff check my account. (see exhibit 3)

6. I had made a Statement to the Police in ██████████████ moved my mobile number to a new account to prevent such visibility. At the time, and until ██████ ████ , I believed this to be the truth, and would have no reason to believe that ██████████ access my call data records.

7. I use the billing platform ███████████ on a daily basis and would not need anyone to review my bill for me.

8. ██████████ has also provided a copy of my file on the ██████████████████ ████████████████ and although this shows marketing emails have been sent to me, there is no record of me calling or email in, or that any information was sent to me at this time (see exhibit 4).

9. My relationship with the Company had broken down completely ██ ██ ██████████ when ████████ refused to supply information requested as a Subject Access Request, and I had asked ██████ to start Court Proceedings for Wrongful and Unfair Dismissal. I would have no desire or need to contact ███████████████████

10. I did not go on holiday until after the Tribunal had taken place, in ████████

11. I asked ██████████████████████ to explain the Company's Position on the processing of my data. I confirmed again that I had upgraded directly with █████████ ████ . (see exhibit 5)

12. This email remains un-answered.

13. In ████████████████ , he has stated that either myself or ██ could easily disprove that I was a ████████████ I supply for clarity the Contract and receipt from ██████████ in ██████████████████████ (see exhibit 6)

14. Equally, if ██████████ had a signed Contract from me, or I had signed a 'Bring your own Device' Policy allowing the Company access to my personal phone records, he would have provided this.

15. The Company failed to supply ██████████████ with this information when requested.

16. The communications between █████████████████████████████ should not have had access to my Call Data Records (see exhibit 7)

**Other relevant matters**

17. On █████████, a reporter ran an article titled 'Are operators doing enough to keep the UK safe?

18. In the article, it questions the legal obligations of the operators under RIPA (Regulations of Investigatory Powers Act) and who can see what? (see exhibit 8)

19. I called ████████ the journalist, and advised him ████ give their Centre of Excellence the same visibility to Call Data Records that the Police can only obtain under RIPA, without the safeguards and security. I explained ██████████ Police's difficulty obtaining information ████ under RIPA, and that PC ████ had to obtain a Court Order to secure the relevant information ████ I explained that the Police have to have just cause and supervisors consent before a request under RIPA is submitted.

20. ████ asked me numerous questions, that I was unsure whether I could answer.

21. I liaised with the Solicitor who acted for me at the Tribunal and asked whether I would be breaking the Court Agreement if I disclosed any information, and he confirmed that I could disclose information regarding the Data Protection breaches, but I should not mention ████ ██████████ reached a Settlement Agreement, as that could possibly cause a problem.

22. I therefore set out a Statement that I supplied ████████ which did not mention ████████ ██████████, that I was a former Employer, that I was dismissed, or that we had agreed a Settlement in ████ ████.

23. I did however disclose that Police Investigation had revealed 115 unauthorised accesses to my personal mobile phone account, and that the Chairman of the Company had been questioned by the Police and denied all knowledge. That a female member of staff was also questioned, and that she stated to the Police that she had not accessed my account, but someone may have used her log in details.

24. I was also able to advise that the ████████████ had processed my data, and breached 6 of the 8 data principles.

25. On or around ██████████ I advised ████████ that the ICO was not going to prosecute any individual for the breaches to DPA.

26. ██████████ contacted █████████████████████████

27. ██████████ both confirmed that they were aware of the Police Investigation against ██████████, and particularly the Chairman ██████████ ████

28. ██████████ emailed me on ██████████ stating that ██████████ called him. Threatening the publication with legal actions and asking if the story had come from me.

29. Obviously, a Reporter protects their sources, although I did say to ███ in a telephone conversation that day that I was happy to confirm the story had come from me, and that I had documentary evidence of everything I had told him.

30. Interestingly, ████████ asked if the 'tip off' had come from a lady, and went on to say that an ex-employee had got the hump and has made a load of false allegations (see exhibit 9)

31. I was able to prove that they were not false allegations by supplying documentary proof, but the publication felt they were unable to report on the matter for fear of legal action against them.

32. In my position at ███████████████████████████████████ whom I had developed an excellent relationship with when I was employed at ████████ ████████████

33. I was aware that the customer was unhappy with ████ coverage and the service received from his account manager.

34. I lent them phones on alternative networks for them to trial for 6-months, and I was notified in ███████████████████████ had instructed they port to the ██ network through EBS (my Employer) when they came out of Contract.

35. I found that four numbers had been signed into a 24-months Contracts, as opposed to 12-months as requested.

36. The customer advised me he had requested ████████ amend the term of the Contract many times, but they had not taken the required action.

37. He asked me to deal with situation, and set me up with an email address at the Company.

38. I emailed ████████ business email address on ████████████████ and asked ████ amend the Contract to the original term. (see exhibit 10)

39. In early ████████████████ emailed the customer as stated that he was aware that ████████████████████████████

40. I then emailed ██ and asked if this was common practice to give out such information (see exhibit 11)

41. ████████████████████ that my email had been forwarded to ████████ ████████████ (see exhibit 12)

42. I have emailed ██████████████████████████████████ to find out if my Call Data Records are still held by the Company. I am expecting a response by the ██ ████████ see exhibit 13).

STATEMENT OF TRUTH

I believe that the facts set out in this Witness Statement are true.

Signed

Name ████████████████

Dated ████████ ███

## [ 5 ]

DATA PROTECTION

I READ A BOOK ON OUR HONEYMOON, THE honeymoon that we went on a few days after my car was painted for the second time.

It was called The Book of You by Claire Kendal and although it was terrifying, it gave me some good ideas. While we were in Thailand, I researched 'Gait Analysis' which is normally used for athletes to improve the distance when running, or change their feet to improve balance. It's a science that can be used to compare CCTV footage to see if the suspect had the same gait. I contacted people from Thailand, I was excited; I thought you won't squirm out of this.

Of course he did, but the threat of it hung over him, and when he failed to supply adequate footage for a comparison to be given, I started to believe the Magistrates would believe me.

I know if I was accused of a crime and I could easily disprove my involvement, I would volunteer all I could.

From: ▓▓▓▓▓▓▓▓▓▓▓▓▓▓▓▓▓▓.co.uk]
Sent: ▓▓▓▓▓▓▓▓▓
To: ▓▓▓▓▓▓▓▓
Subject: ▓▓▓▓▓▓▓▓▓▓

Dear ▓▓▓▓▓▓▓

I write further to your email to me of the ▓▓▓▓▓▓▓▓▓▓▓▓▓ Having taken my Client's instructions, I can confirm he is still willing to offer the personal undertaking to you, as suggested in our previous email. There is no suggestion that my Client has ever contacted you particularly in the last three months therefore a personal undertaking would seem more appropriate and cost effective in line with the Overriding Objectives of the CPR to keep costs to a minimum.

In respect of the undertaking given to the Court, whilst it is accepted that at the time the undertaking was given, both parties anticipated the matter would come to trial before the end of ▓▓▓▓▓ However in light of the recent Case Management Conference and the various directions that

were necessary and the further directions that will be given at the forthcoming Case Management Conference, it is my Client's position that the undertaking to the Court is unnecessary in light of his personal undertaking and is too burdensome. My Client is being excluded from two geographical sights under threat of a penal notice based on interim evidence which has yet to be fully disclosed to him. These restrictions we would suggest are unnecessary in light of the personal undertaking and my Client wishes to see the end of this case and there is little motive for him to jeopardise this.

I note in your emails you have failed to explain what new reasons you feel necessitate the renewal of the undertaking or presumably an application for an interim injunction?

We look forward to hearing from you.

Yours sincerely

From: ▓▓▓▓▓▓▓▓
Sent: ▓▓
To: ▓▓
Subject: ▓▓▓▓▓▓

Mr ▓▓▓▓

Can you please confirm in writing that ▓▓▓▓▓▓▓▓ is not prepared to extend the undertaking to the Court?

Thank you for your email last week, the contents of which are noted.

The relevance of the Payroll Process , payslips and P60's is only relevant as ███████ has claimed in his witness statement dated ███████████, and evidenced in his written statement to the Police (CSS) that I received bonuses he did not approve, and that somehow, ███████████ bonuses without the knowledge of the ████████.

I know the processes in place at the time I left ████████████. It may or not be relevant to the Court to understand the process in place when my salary was paid monthly. It may also be relevant to ask for statements from staff and ex staff in the Payroll Department, HR and Mr ████████████. I will take legal advice as to whether I need to gather this information.

With regard to my request for ████████ to give ████████ to release the information to the ████████ incoming and outgoing data, I thought ████████ would be more comfortable giving DC ████████ access than myself, so included him in the letter, assuming my name and address would be deleted, to protect ████████ personal data. DC ████████ was not aware I had requested the information, as this is part of the civil case, and not the criminal investigation.

Obviously, I am aware of some of the investigatory tools available to the Police but understood Mr ████████ wanted to resolve this issue as speedily as I do. This would be a "quick win" for him. Deputy District ████████ also made it clear to me that I would have to demonstrate to the Court what measures I had taken myself to secure the information before a Production Order would be considered. Requesting the information from ████████ was the obvious first choice.

And whilst this data is not immediately to hand to ████████ would be happy to provide this information upon written request. Having spoken to the Court Disclosure team myself, they would charge only £200 for this information and I would be happy to pay this amount myself if ████████ does agree to send the letter. However, if this is the case, the information should be sent to me, whether via ████████.

Please advise?

████████████
████████████

Dear ████

I write further to your email to me dated ████████████

██ your email to me of the 20th April, you asked for disclosure of the following documents:-

1. ████████████████
   ████████
   ████████████

You will have noted from the Order of the Court dated ████████ that standard disclosure in this matter has been ordered by list on ████████ with inspection and copy documents to be supplied by ████████████. Our Client intends to provide standard disclosure in accordance with the Court Order. However, for us to consider to include the documents you have requested above, can you please state how these documents are relevant to your case in accordance with CPR 31.6. A copy of the CPR can be found on the www.justice.gov.uk website. Specifically we fail to see what relevance the payroll process", your payslips and P60s are to either party's case.

Further, part of your request relates to documents which may not be in our Client's control, therefore you are urged to seek legal advice in respect of this and to investigate the possibility of a third party disclosure Order. In addition to this, we are concerned that you state that the disclosure you seek is somehow to assist DC ████████, presumably with his investigations. As you will be aware the police have wide ranging investigatory powers under the Police and Criminal Evidence Act 1984. If they wish to seek this information from either my Client or ████████ do so themselves. We will be writing to ████████ separately to put our concerns to them, as my Client has assisted them with all of their enquiries and we are concerned further requests are being made through you and not to us or our Client directly.

Finally we note the enquiry in your email as to whether our Client was willing to extend the undertaking given to the Court at the return hearing. I can confirm our Client is willing to extend his personal undertaking to you directly, along the terms given to the Court at the return hearing.

Yours sincerely,

████████████████

From: ████████████ 36
To: ████████████

M█

I received further papers from the Court on Friday, which has the ████████████

Can you please advise by ███████████████████████ is prepared to extend the undertaking, or I will make a further Application to the Court?

I await your comments as to whether ████████ is prepared to give permission in relation to the CDR's, as requested. As I have had no response from you regarding this, I have now explored relevant experts, and have amended the letter for ████████ accordingly.

Would it be reasonable to suggest that you take your clients instruction on all matters by ██████ ██████

████████████████

██████████████████████

## [ 6 ]

THE C.P.S

IT IS WELL DOCUMENTED AND WELL REPORTED THAT I am highly critical of some parts of the CPS.

Please don't get me wrong, there are some amazing people making really tough decisions working there. The two gentlemen I met and spoke with from London were totally amazing in what was horrible circumstances, but at least they listened to me and agreed to continue with the case.

My problem though is that, because it took so long to get to the point where the charges were re-instated, they were outside of the Statute of Limitation to charge him with stalking, so in all intense and purpose, he got away with the seriousness of the crime, and stood trial for two counts of criminal damage.

I have been criticised for speaking to the press, and will be again when the book hits the stands, but I really don't care. What is more important to me is raising awareness what stalking really is, and it isn't just someone hanging around outside your house, or unrequited love.

It is brutal, it is mean, it affects every aspect of your life, and of those around you. People have asked me why I didn't ask my husband or any number of people 'to have a word with him', but it was really important to me that I didn't sink to his level, and although frustrating at times, I still believe I took the best route.

That is not to say that my husband didn't want to. I can't tell you how many arguments we had on the subject, especially when I was frustrated or scared. It got to the stage where I felt I had to stop telling my husband everything, because he got so angry, I was scared he would thump him, and that would be 'game over' for the moral high-ground. There have been many a night when I have physically had to sit on him to prevent him from leaving the house, but my argument always won.

I still believe that the two of them would have got into a fight, and if my husband was arrested, I would have been left un-protected whilst he was held. But I do understand his need to want to find a solution, and I will always thank him for allowing me to do this my way.

The police have repeatedly told me 'it's a civil matter', and sometimes there is a case through civil remedies, but more often than not the Police have got it wrong. Today was another case in point. See your solicitor I have been advised. No, I will see the Chief Constable and then my solicitor. Why in 2019 do they not understand that stalking isn't just a civil case? I think it is lack of training and understanding. I have dialled 999 and no one has come. I have dialled 999 and been told not to shout at the operator. The thing is, I never shout or raise my voice, but I am extremely assertive, and some people just cannot handle that, especially I think, coming from a woman. #metoo.

So to Simon and Eduardo, thank you. Thank you for believing me, believing that we could win, because we did. And for a brief time, my faith in the British Justice system was restored, but unfortunately, it didn't last. These people are playing Russian Roulette with our lives. And I will not accept that anyone has that much power over my life. Who has decided that my life doesn't matter?

From: ███████████████████████████
Date: ████████████████████████████████
To: ███████████████████
Subject: ███████████████████████████
Reply-To ████████████████████████

Good afternoon

Thank you for your letter, received today.

My email address for correspondence is
████████████████████████ and my mobile number is ████

The Judge I have referenced in my papers is ████████████
and he was most surprised to see ██████████ in Court on the
morning I actually gave my evidence, and mentioned it in front
of the Jury. He had heard my case in the civil court on
████████ and made it clear that if ███████ did not
voluntarily give he Court an Undertaking he would issue an
Injunction, and I feel it would be beneficial for you to get a
Judicial opinion and think he would be a good reference point
for your consideration.

████████████████████████████████████████████████████████
████████████████████████████████████████████████████████

███████████████ lies to the Police and to the Courts, and PC
████████████████████████████ and DC ███████████████████
or ████████████████████████████████████████ I believe
█████████████ will also confirm that his perjury were proven
in both case, in which he has been involved.  He would also be
able to confirm that in the trial of ████████████ he heard
evidence of a threat being made by █████████████████████ in ██
██████ and again in ███████████████████

Without any witnesses, of which there are many who could
confirm bad character, it would be a very short trial.

Whilst ████████ is a compulsive liar, and avoids detection by
simply disguising himself, I firmly believe that given all of
the evidence, a Jury would convict.

The Police have never searched his properties, or computer,
yet I have told them he is clearly monitoring my movements and
activity on social media.

I do understand that the CPS have to think in precedents,
however, unless challenged, how are new precedents ever made?

Stalking is established, and if there is any doubt that my
life is in danger, he should, in my opinion, answer to the
Courts.

Please do not hesitate to contact me if you require any
additional information.

CPS ████████████

Victims Review

████████

Dear Sir/Madam

CASE REFERENCE ████████████████████

I wish to appeal against the Crown Prosecution Services decision to discontinue actions against ███████████████████████ in two counts of Criminal Damage.

████████ has subjected me to a course of conduct that can only be seen as Stalking, and the criminal damage was just a part of the continued campaign.

I was employed by the defendant at ████████████████████████████████ until my dismissal in ████████

Prior to my dismissal, the ██████████ was dismissed and arrested for Fraud, and his trial begins on ████████████████ and I am a witness for the defence.

After I left the Company, I met with the ████████████████████ where it became apparent he was accessing my personal mobile phone account. Unbeknown to me, the 'off the record' conversation was recorded, and an audio recording was supplied to DC ████████████ of ████████████████

In ████████████ I met with DC ████████████████ and gave a statement in relation to the accusations against ████████

I made a statement to ████████████████████████████████████ was the investigating officer) ████████ was questioned by the Police on ████████ where he denied accessing my account. However, the Police did have the transcript of the audio recording where ████████ s heard talking to a female ████████████████████████████████ ████████ where is states that 'he didn't tell me he had my phone records on him when we met. (attached 1).

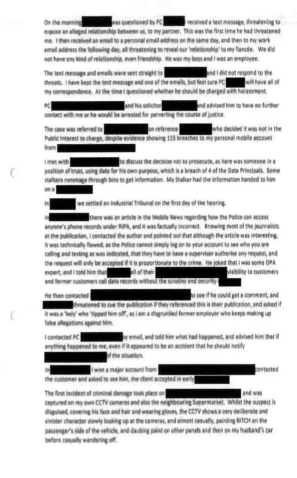

On the morning ████ was questioned by PC ████ received a text message, threatening to expose an alleged relationship between us, to my partner. This was the first time he had threatened me. I then received an email to a personal email address on the same day, and then to my work email address the following day, all threatening to reveal our 'relationship' to my fiancée. We did not have any kind of relationship, even friendship. He was my boss and I was an employee.

The text message and emails were sent straight to ████ and I did not respond to the threats. I have kept the text message and one of the emails, but feel sure PC ████ will have all of my correspondence. At the time I questioned whether he should be charged with harassment.

PC ████ and his solicitor ████ and advised him to have no further contact with me or he would be arrested for perverting the course of justice.

The case was referred to ████ on reference ████ who decided it was not in the Public Interest to charge, despite evidence showing 115 breaches to my personal mobile account from ████

I met with ████ to discuss the decision not to prosecute, as here was someone in a position of trust, using data for his own purpose, which is a breach of 4 of the Data Principals. Some stalkers rummage through bins to get information. My Stalker had the information handed to him on a ████

In ████ we settled an Industrial Tribunal on the first day of the hearing.

In ████ there was an article in the Mobile News regarding how the Police can access anyone's phone records under RIPA, and it was factually incorrect. Knowing most of the journalists at the publication, I contacted the author and pointed out that although the article was interesting, it was technically flawed, as the Police cannot simply log on to your account to see who you are calling and texting as was indicated, that they have to have a supervisor authorise any request, and the request will only be accepted if it is proportionate to the crime. He joked that I was some DPA expert, and I told him that ████ all of their ████ visibility to customers and former customers call data records without the scrutiny and security

He then contacted ████ to see if he could get a comment, and ████ threatened to sue the publication if they referenced this is their publication, and asked if it was a 'lady' who 'tipped him off', as I am a disgruntled former employer who keeps making up false allegations against him.

I contacted PC ████ by email, and told him what had happened, and advised him that if anything happened to me, even if it appeared to be an accident that he should notify ████ of the situation.

In ████ I won a major account from ████ contacted the customer and asked to see him, the client accepted in early ████

The first incident of criminal damage took place on ████ and was captured on my own CCTV cameras and also the neighbouring Supermarket. Whilst the suspect is disguised, covering his face and hair and wearing gloves, the CCTV shows a very deliberate and sinister character slowly looking up at the cameras, and almost casually, painting BITCH on the passenger's side of the vehicle, and daubing paint on other panels and then on my husband's car before casually wandering off.

Having known ██████████████ I had no hesitation identifying ███████████████ as the offender. Although he had covered his face, I recognised his walk, the way he holds his hands, and his general gait.

On ██████ I received a text message from an unknown ███ mobile, that said Revenge is sweet with patience, time to strike back, watch your back lady, I'm coming for you.

It was clear that the same person who had painted by car was also responsible for the text message.

The use of the word 'lady' so soon after he had asked the journalist if it was a 'lady' who tipped him off spoke volumes. Most people would ask if it was male or female.

I visited ████████████ station with my phone and spoke to an officer who explained that they were going off duty for the day, and would be busy the following day, but would arrest ███████ n ████████████ This never happened, or they would have probably found him with the phone, either in his car or on his person.

Two further messages followed, and then ███████ visited the client on, I believe, the ████████ He basically went in to defame my character, with his opening line being 'we had a problem with ███████'. The client stopped him and asked whether he had anything to tell him had any reflection on my ability to do my job, which is managing his mobile phone account. As he had promoted me to the ████████████████ he could not continue in the vein he had intended, and my client said that perhaps he should be asking why they lost the business rather than 'slag me off'.

I thought that having heard this, it would be the end of it, but I was wrong, and my car was painted again on ████████████ again the same offender was caught on CCTV. I went on my honeymoon, but it was ruined, as I was anxious the whole time we were away. I returned to work on the ████████ and I received the 'still watching and waiting' text the following day.

The Police file was then passed to ███████████████████████████ s the investigating officer.

We met on, I believe, ██████████ and some two weeks later, DC ███████ arranged for 5 Police officers from ███████████████ to visit the offices of ██████████████████ and the thought was two would search the business premises, two his home, and one would take him into custody.

However, when the officers arrived, they were advised that ███████████████████████
████████

Knowing he would be notified of the attendance, I represented myself in Court and secured an ex-parte injunction on ████████████ as I was terrified he would harm me once he got home.

The papers were served on ███ when he arrived home on the ████████████ and he contacted ████████████ to arrange an interview on the ████████

He denied knowledge of any involvement, suggested that I sent the text messages to myself in order to discredit him, and stated that he had seen photographs on Facebook that ████████ had visited my home, and that I had received bonuses I was not entitled to.

The Police has subsequently advised me that some of the text messages were sent from ████████ but I was in ████████████ when 3 of the 4 messages were received, and I called ████ from my mobile on at least two occasions and the work phone once. All of this can be verified, but another deliberate attempt to discredit me to the Police.

In the return hearing at the Court on ████████████ provided evidence that ███████
continued to pay revenue on my mobile phone number until the day I ported, even though I was not
a customer of ████████████████ He said that this proved I was a customer, but did not
provide a Contract, receipt or any other proof, where I had proved to the Court that I had upgraded
directly with the ██████████████████ advised the ICO that my number
was on the incorrect connector code and this allowed ███ to monitor who I called or text.

I challenged ██████ anyone had accessed my account from ████████████████
█████ and they confirmed that they account had been accessed by someone at ██████████
████████ on one date, but a number of occasions on this date. (attached 2).

████████ has repeatedly lied to the Police, denying knowledge that my account had been
accessed, despite his own audio recording that confirmed he had my call data records with him
when we met.  He lied when he stated that I received bonuses I was not entitled to and again, I
believe this was a deliberate attempt to discredit me to the Police.  He refused to answer why his car
was caught on APNR cameras 13 minutes before each incidence of criminal damage, less than a mile
from my home.

According to the Police, the CPS have decided to drop charges as they do not feel there is more than
a 50% chance of winning the case.

**The Strengths of the case.**

Motive – there is a clear motive for ██████ behaviour

CCTV – although the footage is not clear, I have 100% identified ██████

ANPR – his vehicle was approximately 17 miles away from his home at 2.30 am on each occasion of
criminal damage.

**The Weakness of the case**

CCTV – the CPS do not believe his gait is recognisable.  CCTV from the Supermarket of ██████
was never collected.

No eyewitnesses – to my knowledge, my neighbour or the flats overlooking the house were not
canvassed.

APNR – no image of the driver

No forensic evidence – no evidence was ever taken from my home, and to my knowledge neither his
home nor business premises were ever searched.

The defendant offered no explanation as to why his vehicle was caught on Police camera's some 15
and a half miles from my home, at 2.17 am on each occasion of criminal damage to my vehicles, and
the CPS don't think this needs answering?  If he resided in ██████ and his vehicle was caught on
camera, it would still be suspicious, but I am sure a jury should be given the opportunity to hear
from the Police and from him.

I also believe the decision is based on the offenders wealth and that he will be able to afford the best defence lawyers money can buy, and believe that if he was on a wage, and could not afford such a luxury, the decision would be different, and if this is correct, makes a mockery of them claim that the CPS 'Championing justice and defending the rights of victims, fairly, firmly and effectively is at the heart of all we do'.

The Police notified me in August that they were going to charge ████ with two counts of criminal damage. I now understand that he was summons to appear in Court on ██████ to answer charges, but this will not proceed.

Please see the Supporting letter from the National Stalking Advocacy Service, Paladin, that has made an assessment of the facts, and have decided that I am at high risk of harm at the hands of ████

Characteristics of a Stalker, that also apply to ██████ behaviour

Gathering information on the victim

Defamation of character

Objectification

Threats of violence

Cyberstalking

Isolation

Surveillance

In the civil case, ██████ references the CPS's decision not to prosecute the data protection offences as 'a failed complaint', and he already thinks he is cleverer than the Police, and that he is above the law. Approximately 15 years ago, he was stopped, driving at nearly 100 miles an hour, I think it was a ████████ Several days later, he was involved in a Police chase whilst speeding. To avoid detection, he drove the wrong way up a slip round, and the wrong way round a roundabout, and managed to escape.

As the Police managed to get a partial plate, he was questioned, denied the offence, and then boasted to everyone that he out smarts and out thinks the Police.

The civil case against ████ has been heard at ██████████ I can supply you all of the documentation presented in the case. If you would rather get it from the Court directly, the case reference is ████ During the trial, ████ has shown total contempt for the Court, by lying to the Court and presenting a fabrication of lies.

████ solicitor, ██████████ advised my Barrister in ████ that his client was an extremely wealthy man, who could afford to fight my efforts and questioned whether I had the funds to see the action through. I know that ████ would have continued to fight the action, regardless of the financial cost to him if he was innocent, and although I have failed to agree to any of his ridiculous demands, and told his solicitor I was happy to take my chances with the Court, he still agreed to give the Undertaking, without terms attached.

When I was employed as the ███████████████ view was to fight any Industrial Tribunal, regardless of the cost. He would rather spend £20,000, than settle for £2,000, and I can recall one case where the ██████████████ had to cajole ███████ in settling a racial discrimination case rather than allowing it to proceed to the hearing.

In another instance, he called someone in who was off sick, to sack them. When I discovered his intention, I questioned him as to whether he had notified the staff member that they were coming in to a disciplinary action which could result in their dismissal, with the adequate notice, and the invitation to invite a colleague. He had not, and said he didn't need to; his belief affirmed that he could do what he wanted. I asked him to reconsider, as he would hand the staff member a guaranteed award if he continued in this vein, as it would be me who had to stand at the Tribunal.

Eventually, he calmed down, and the meeting went ahead without a dismissal.

Whilst I was employed, I became aware of a character he calls ████████████ He advised the Senior Management team that ███████ had been out collecting a debt with an iron bar. When he was questioned about this, he joked that he was ███████ During my employment, ███████ came out occasionally, and I witnessed him trying to start fights with competitors on two separate occasions and witnessed him break ███████████ nose at a Christmas Party and then drive home blind drunk.

When I was dismisses, I requested information as a Subject Access Request. I waited over 40 days before contacting him again, and his responded that he did not see the relevance of the information, and would not supply it. I responded to say that it was not for him to understand the relevance, but to supply it in accordance with the SAR. He came back to me and said that he can decide what he likes. All of this is documented, and again shows a complete arrogance for the rules and laws that the rest of us adhere to.

His own staff and personal friends have not been surprised by his actions, and one particular close friend was not aware of any of the allegations against him. There comments to me were that if he was innocent, he would have told them what was happening, but would have said I was lying. His silence to those closest to him speaks volumes to those who know him well.

Staff at ████████████████ have been advised not to talk to me, or have any contact with me, or it could lead to their dismissal. As some of the current and former employees are personal friends of mine, I believe his intention is to isolate me from a support structure.

He spoke to one of my former colleagues, and a close personal friend of mine ███████ She has also known him for over 17 years, having worked for him at Senior Management level. He accused her of trying to destroy his business, with her (me). She said he spoke with such venom that she was actually shocked, and has felt scared for me ever since. She has said it was clear he hated her, but she has never heard him 'lose it' so badly in all the years she has known him. He seems to hold me responsible for everything that is going wrong in his business.

I am not the only member of staff that has left the business and won business from his business, but to my knowledge, I am the only person who he has targeted in this way. He has sacked or lost a lot of staff members who have stayed in the industry, but it is possible that I had access to more customers in my position of Sales Manager. The fact that I visited customers when there was a real problem, and I solved the problems quickly and efficiently would definitely be one of the reasons customers are coming to me when they are out of Contract. ███████ also have a massive turnover of staff, and customers are unhappy with the service they receive.

However, one person cannot be responsible for everything that is going wrong, and the fact that he attributes all of the blame to me proves he is delusional.

He was recently in Court on a separate issue, and had to be advised by the Judge that he was contradicting his own statement; further proof that he is an unsafe witness, and will 'trip himself' up in his fabrication of lies.

I understand that the CPS need a reasonable prospect of conviction. However, no one has ever been approached by the Police, despite me giving details of people who know him, will probably identify him from the CCTV, and can confirm 'bad character'.

The negotiations between his solicitor and myself have confirmed that somehow, he is continuing to view my online presence, and was concerned that he would be 'vilified on Facebook'. I have blocked him and his family members, and defriended anyone who could potentially show him anything I post.

He has given a 17 month undertaking to the Court, however, this is unlikely to prevent him in the future if he decides to come for me again. I understand a restraining order can be given by the Court even on an acquittal, and therefore I believe this case should be heard, in its entirety, and not the criminal damage charges in isolation. I believe he would be more inclined to moderate his behaviour if there was a restraining order in place where he could face serious, life changing sanctions if broken.

I also firmly believe that if he is not held accountable for his actions, his belief that he is above the law will only be embedded further, and it will corroborate his belief that he is entitled to behave the way he does towards me.

Viewing me as weak or lesser may support his delusions that I need to be punished, and I seriously believe he will cause me harm or possibly death. Two thirds of stalkers will damage their victim's property. Property damage may be associated with rage, revenge or a desire to harm something the victim cares about, and often precedes physical attacks.

The Police arranged to have the fire department visit my home, and fit fire extinguishers and a lockable flat for my letterbox. Crime Prevention have also fitted anti grab strips to my 6 foot garden wall, and anti-vandal paint. I have fitted alarms to every downstairs window, have internal door locks on every internal door, which are locked when I am out or at night. I have spent over £5,000 updating and improving my CCTV, which now have 8 camera's covering the house and garden, with a monitor at the front door so I can see that there is no one outside the house before I leave, and my house alarm has been improved to include panic alarms.

I take regular one to one self-defence classes, and carry a personal alarm and a Farb Gel Spray.

I drive alternate routes to and from work, check my vehicle and lock the doors once inside. I am mindful of other traffic, although knowing all of the vehicles he has access to within his business is impossible. I am also aware he may use some of the wealth his solicitor boasts over to hire someone to do his dirty work.

Can I also remind you of the Protocol on the appropriate handling of stalking offences between the CPS and ACPO?

The purpose of the Protocol is to:

- Reflect National Policing and CPS policy;
- Ensure a robust and appropriate criminal justice response to stalking
- Establish an early and effective liaison between the Police and the CPS in stalking cases
- Achieve improvement and consistent performance in the investigation and prosecution of stalking offences
- Improve the service to victims of stalking and increase public confidence more widely in the ability of the Criminal Justice System to deal with stalking cases.

My own case so far does not reflect any of the above.

I would ask you to seriously consider the decision of the CPS not to pursue my complaint, and if possible, to consider action to the wider case that is stalking.

Yours faithfully

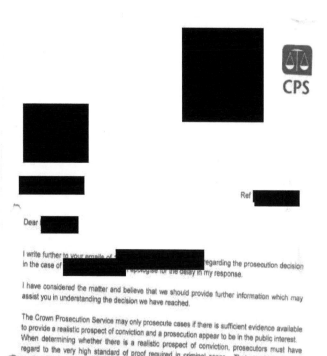

I write further to your emails of ████████████████████ regarding the prosecution decision in the case of ████████████████████ ████████ I apologise for the delay in my response.

I have considered the matter and believe that we should provide further information which may assist you in understanding the decision we have reached.

The Crown Prosecution Service may only prosecute cases if there is sufficient evidence available to provide a realistic prospect of conviction and a prosecution appear to be in the public interest. When determining whether there is a realistic prospect of conviction, prosecutors must have regard to the very high standard of proof required in criminal cases. That standard of proof requires that a court must be 'satisfied so as to be sure' of guilt before it can convict a defendant. In addition, the burden of proving the case to that standard falls upon the prosecution, with the defendant generally being required to prove nothing at all.

In essence, the evidence provided to us by the police consisted of the video recordings of your car being damaged, the history of your involvement with ████████ which could be said to provide a motive for him to cause the damage, your opinion that the person shown upon the recording was ████████ and information from the police concerning the sighting of a vehicle registered to ████████████████ at the material times.

Whilst it is accepted that ████████ is a person whose appearance and mannerisms are very familiar to you, the lawyer who reviewed the case against him concluded that the nature and quality of the recording were such as to prevent a positive identification to be made from it. In particular she took the view that the mannerisms of the person shown were not so distinctive as to be able to persuade a court that ███████ could be identified by them.

The sighting of a car registered to ███████ in the area was deeply suspicious, but not by itself sufficient to allow us to prove the case, particularly given that the driver cannot be identified from the images taken of the vehicle.

The view of the evidence taken collectively was that it provided a very strong suspicion that ██ ███████ was responsible for the damage to your vehicle, but fell short of placing us in a position where we could say that there was a realistic prospect of us proving the case to the very high standard referred to above.

I hope that this letter further assists you in understanding what has happened in this case and how the CPS came to the decision to bring the prosecution to an end.

If you would still like us to conduct a full review of the decision, please contact the CPS Appeals and Review Unit at RightToReview@cps.gsi.gov.uk by ███████████.

District Crown Prosecutor

INVESTORS
IN PEOPLE

PRIVATE

Dear ███████

**Victims' Right to Review (VRR) Scheme request in the case of** ████████████

I am writing to you as the specialist Senior Crown Advocate dealing with this matter, following your request for a formal review under the VRR scheme of the decision of the Crown Prosecution Service ██████████ not to proceed with a prosecution in this case.

At this stage my review is not complete. In order to reach a final decision it is necessary, in my opinion, for me to clarify several aspects of the evidence. There is further work that I would ask the police to undertake if my decision were to be that charges should be brought, but at this stage I need to clarify your evidence. Rather than ask the officer to take another statement, I have concluded that the most appropriate course is for a pre-trial witness interview.

The interview shall be with you and conducted by me. It shall be recorded so that, if the case does proceed to charges, the contents of our interview may be disclosed to ████████ lawyers. There may be another CPS employee to assist in taking a note. You may bring a supporter to the interview if you wish and subject to me agreeing that is an appropriate person; any supporter should not be a potential witness in this or any connected case, which would exclude anyone who knows ████

The purpose of the interview is to enable me to focus on and clarify the identification of ███████ as the offender that you have already made to police officers. It should take no more than an hour. It will take place either at a convenient police station or CPS office on a date to be arranged.

At the end of the interview I shall not be able to provide you with my final decision on whether █ ███████ should be charged as I will need further time to reflect and draft my advice. I appreciate that this further delay shall be frustrating when it concerns events that took place over 1 year ago, but it an essential stage in the decision making process. ████████

There is no compulsion on you to attend the interview and if you do have any reservations or queries, please contact me in advance.

My commitments in appeal courts and other professional engagements mean that I shall not be able to meet you until the week commencing ███████ at the earliest. I would be grateful if you could email my colleagues at rightforreview@cps.gsi.gov.uk to indicate whether you are willing to attend such an interview and, if so, which dates & times may be most convenient for you; we shall then confirm the availability of an appropriate venue and write again to finalise the details.

It is because of the need for an interview that the review has not yet been completed. I would expect to be able to inform you of the final outcome of this review within 28 days of our interview.

Yours sincerely

**CPS**

Dear

<u>Victims' Right to Review (VRR) Scheme request in the case of</u>

Further to our letter dated ▇▇▇▇▇▇▇▇ I am now writing to provide you with an update as to the progress of this important matter.

In our last letter we indicated that in accordance with your request, your case would be fully reviewed and we would make every effort to give you a response within 28 days.

Unfortunately, it has not been possible to complete the review within 28 days because the specialist prosecutor requires further time in order to analyse the meeting notes which was held in ▇▇▇▇▇▇

The Specialist Prosecutor will contact you as soon as the review has been completed and a final decision has been reached. If this is not completed within the next 28 days, you will be provided with a further update.

I do apologise that the review of your case is taking longer than anticipated but this matter is very important and it is essential that the final decision is made after a careful and independent

# [ 7 ]

THE CHIEF CONSTABLE

WHEN THE CHIEF CONSTABLE IGNORED THE LETTER
below, he 'tweeted' that he was visiting the theatre to
judge a competition.

I responded to the tweet that I would see him there. It
was a beautiful, hot day and I left work early. As I
pulled into the area, a police car followed me. I
thought I was going to be arrested. I wasn't. I left my
handbag in the boot of my car, taking with me just a
mobile phone (I carry two on different networks so I
am never out of contact). I spoke to officers and asked
what time their boss would arrive. They didn't know
he was going to the event, and some legged it back to
their cars to get dressed properly.

I saw him arrive, and as he walked towards me, I
addressed him. He is a really tall chap, and quite
intimidating, but I stuck my hand out to shake his and
introduced myself. I explained who I was and that I

had sent him an email and he hadn't acknowledged it and that I wanted him to see who I was so if anything happened to me 'on his watch' I wanted him to be responsible, and that he would see my face when he closed his eyes at night. I felt it was really important to get in front of him, so at least if something did happen, he would have met me. I got nothing from him. I do not think he would have given a damn.

I was delighted when he moved on.

I am, however, less than impressed with our current Chief Constable and the (mis) handling of many cases including the case of Harry Dunn, the teenager who tragically died in a road traffic accident with the other driver fleeing the scene using diplomatic immunity for her avoidance of prosecution.

His since deleted tweet when the family announced they were to sue was an absolute disgrace and the Justice4Harry campaign proved, yet again, when you are dealing with the worst pain in your life, you still have to fight to make people accountable.

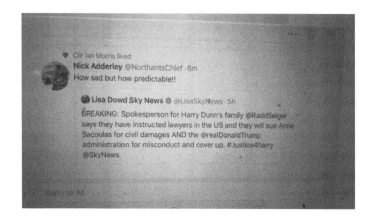

This was my letter to the aforementioned gentleman.

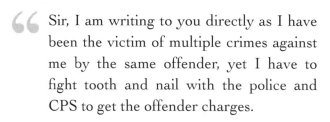

> Sir, I am writing to you directly as I have been the victim of multiple crimes against me by the same offender, yet I have to fight tooth and nail with the police and CPS to get the offender charges.

> I was employed as sales manager at a communications company from March 2008 until 24<sup>th</sup> October 2013, when I was dismissed for having contact with a former employee. My former employer boasted to me that he was accessing my call records. The local police have a copy of the transcript from an 'off the record' meeting I had with him on 1<sup>st</sup> November 2013. He recorded the meeting and another director gave the DC a copy of

the recording. I have seen the transcript of another conversation he had with the HR manager, where he states that he didn't tell me that he had his phone records on him.

The police established 115 breaches to my personal data during a six-month period in 2013. 68 further breaches were discovered in 2014. No one was charged, as it was not in the public interest. The person who breached my data worked for a business with in excess of 42,000 mobile phone numbers and approximately 20,000 landline numbers. Their clients included solicitors, professional sports stars and household name brands.

On the day that the defendant was questioned by the police, he sent me a threatening text message, threatening to expose our true relationship to my then fiancé. When he got no response, he went on to send an email to a personal email address, and the following day, to my work email address. All were sent to the police who contacted the defendant and advised him not to contact me.

In June 2014, an industrial tribunal was listed for 2 days. We reached a settlement figure of £33,500, which was paid to me, most of which was tax free.

In, I think December 2014, I spoke to a journalist who wrote an article about the police abusing RIPA and getting access to call data records. I spoke to this reporter, and advised him that certain mobile phone companies give partners the kind of access that the police would welcome, without any of the scrutiny and security that the police have to go through. He contacted me, and after I spoke to my solicitor, I was able to tell him about the 115 breaches to my personal data. I did not give him the name of the company, but he saw where I had previously worked, and contacted individuals for a comment. The defendant threatened to sue them if they published. They are a small publication, and didn't proceed with the story. He asked the publication if it was a 'lady' who tipped them off, and said I was a bitter former employer who keeps making up false allegations against him. I am mindful that anything I do or say, he will sue for defamation, and therefore make sure I have evidence to support what I say.

Around the same time, I won a major account from a communications company. The defendant visited the client, his only objective to discredit me. He failed, but I was concerned and contacted the police by email to say that if anything happened to me, even if it was an accident, then to find out Baker's whereabouts. I became aware when I worked for him, that he had an 'alter ego' that he called by another name. This 'Hyde' dressed as a skin head and liked to hurt people. The defendant had been in the Royal Navy and liked to boast that he 'knew' people.

He then took it upon himself the paint BITCH down the side of my car. I don't dispute I have become hostile and angry over the past 4-years. A month later, he returned and threw red paint over my car. I also received threatening text messages from a burner phone that could never be attributed to the defendant, but I have no doubt that he sent the messages because of the language used.

In March 2015, five police officers attended the offices of my former place of employment. The intention was to take the defendant into custody, search his home and his office for the phone. When they arrived, they were told he had gone on holiday and wouldn't return to work until March.

Fearing for my safety, I managed to secure an ex-parte injunction. I telephoned his mobile number (withholding my number of course) to ensure he was back in the country. No foreign ring tone told me he was back. I then rang his house phone, and established that he was at home. I then arranged for the process server to serve papers on him.

He was not permitted to come within 50 metres of my home or business. Eventually, after a lot of league arguments, I managed to secure a 17-month undertaking that has now expired.

After the defendant painted BITCH down the side of my car, my solicitor emailed the firm that represented him during the tribunal and advised of the breach to the settlement agreement. His solicitors argued that the injunction had been over turned.

The defendant was summons to appear in Court to answer charges of 2 counts of criminal damage, but the CPS withdrew the charges.

I appealed, met for a pre-trial witness interview and the CPS (London) concluded that the charges should not have been dropped.

I successfully managed to secure a conviction in January 2017, and was given a lifetime restraining order.

Local news ran an article on the case, *Former Essentiall Owner Found Guilty*. Finally I could let people know who it was who had been harassing, intimidating, and indeed stalking me.

I sent emails to a lot of local businesses from my work email address, the article had a really good photograph of him, and I believed the more people knew what had happened to me the safer I would be.

His solicitors then wrote to me directly threatening legal action as I had broken the terms of the settlement agreement. I saw my solicitor who advised me that I had not broken the terms of the Settlement Agreement, that the defendant had broken it in a repudiatory fashion. A fundament breach of a contract, sometimes known as a repudiatory breach is a breach so fundamental that it permits the distressed party to terminate performance of the contract, in addition, entitling that party to sue for damages.

In February 2017, I went to the United States for a few days, and when I got back, found out he had appealed against the conviction.

The police, the CPS nor the Court have contacted me regarding the date, but I have found out it is being heard in August 2017.

Although the defendant has announced to the press his retirement, he is still the majority shareholder of the business. If you go onto the company web site, he is still listed as the Chairman. If you go onto Companies House's website, you can download the Share Holder Agreement that states very clearly that the Board of Directors can do nothing without the defendant's permission.

DC Andrew Barnes contacted me to say that although the CPS say there is a 'technical' breach, it is not in the public interest to prosecute. I have asked time and time again, what is the point of a restraining order if the police are not going to police it when it is broken? No-one has yet given me an answer. Last week, on Thursday to be precise, I was advised that the review into the decision not to prosecute had been concluded and I would receive a letter. Yesterday, I chased the letter, only to be told that my file is under review. No explanation for the delay. I just have to accept it!

At the hands of your police force, I have been told I cannot make an appointment to see a police officer. I have been fobbed off from the control room and sent to the Magistrates Court, I have been given incorrect advice and now the decision has been delayed, for how long, no one can or will tell me.

Do you think this is good enough, Sir? As the victim, let me say, it doesn't feel good enough.

When you read this, do you still feel as proud of the police force you control?

So, this is my story, and this is how I think you can do better in the future.

When a crime is reported, ask the caller if they can go to their local station to make a statement?

So much police time is wasted driving around the county to take a statement when a massive percentage of people would be happy to make an appointment if it is explained to them that the time saved will be used to investigate. If the caller is particularly articulate, they could be asked to email the complaint in, and someone can make it into a statement and leave it on the front desk for signature. Obviously, you are going to have to go out sometimes, not every-one has the capacity to do this, but the one size fits all approach is wasting valuable resources.

Why have trained officers taking statements? Why can't the PHSO do this? Or the Specials? Or even an administrator? Hours of police officers time is being wasted, going in two's to lone females houses, when the complainant might be more comfortable sitting at the police station with an administrator.

I have written many statements in my life and I do not need a DC to travel to my home wasting 20 minutes each way, and an hour or two writing a statement I and a lot of others, are completely able to do? We all use emails. Send victims a template so the format is correct.

I wanted to join the police force in 1985, but a back operation at the age of 12 prevented me from being able to. I am sure though that your officers want to police, they want to investigate, they want to catch the bad guys – free up their time to do so.

In the real world, we have a Client Relationship System (CRM) and every single client is logged on their, and even if I am out of the office, my colleagues can see the last action and conversation I had, the time and date. Nowadays, you can even file a call recording to the client. Why not operate something similar? If I need an update, and my officers is on a rest day, or on holiday, no one else can help me. What a far better experience it would be for me to call in, and find out where the case is at, rather than wait for Scott to call me back.

Stop over-promising and under delivering. Why offer enhanced care when I have never received this. I don't need it but why state that because I am the victim of multiple crimes, I will receive better care.

Ask your 'customers' how your force is

doing. Listen to the feedback and make the necessary changes. I am happy to help with this. Customer Satisfaction Surveys are a part of my world. Perhaps you should adopt something similar.

Allow victims to see police officers when they have got a complaint, or want a decision reviewing. So much time must be spend reading a file, but I could some it up in half an hour. Obviously I would have to wait for the decision as legal teams must offer advice, but when I have complained, a big wall is put up, and I can't speak to anyone. This is when I want to see a police officer.

Speak to the other forces. There is currently an investigation into the defendant and A.N Other by local police for Fraud and Perjury. Speak to each other and the CPS. These people make stories up about people. They lie. They discredit. They ruin people's lives.

I offered to pay for gait analysis. I have offered the services of my solicitor. I have offered to get someone in who understands the company set up's to explain why the restraining order was broken. None of these offers have been taken up. It is in my interest for him to be prosecuted for the breach to the restraining order. The appeal is unlikely to go ahead if he is arrested and has to explain himself to the Magistrates why he thinks it is acceptable to contact me, albeit indirectly.

Understand stalking. With the emergence of social media, stalkers don't just hang around your house, as I have been told by a police officer. Stalkers can hack emails, mobile phones, call data records. It's just as intimidating not to know if every email you sent is being viewed. No different from going through my knicker draw.

Sir, I have spent £15,000 of my own money protecting myself, my home, my place of work. I felt safer in America than I feel in my own home and that is a very sad indictment on your policing.

## [ 8 ]

PREVENTION

I AM LEARNING THIS AS I GO ALONG, SO PLEASE accept my apologies if I forget something.

The psyche of a stalker, a domestic abuser, a bully, they are very similar. Most are narcissists, psychopaths, sociopaths, control freaks and many more. I am not trained, but I have consulted professionals in this area, and this was the overall feeling.

Keep a diary, record times, dates and places and the incidents and how they made you feel. It only requires two incidence of feeling harassed or intimidated for stalking to be considered, although the reality is that this is not always the case.

If you are in danger, or fear you will be attacked, dial 999 immediately. The police would rather spend time checking your surroundings and ensuring you are safe than investigating your murder.

If you cannot reach someone and you fear from them, the police will do a welfare check, for exactly the same reason, whether it is fear of someone else's actions or their own.

## SOCIAL MEDIA

Block your stalker and set your privacy settings to the highest level, and keep checking them.

Sometimes you want to make something public such as a missing person post, but remember to make sure they are private before you post anything again. Defriend mutual friends is also advisable unless you know 100% you can trust them. I found out some of my 'friends' were sharing my posts with him and some of his 'friends' were sharing with me too.

Don't allow anyone to 'tag' you into photos where they share your location. You may as well invite them along to join you.

Change your name. You can be known as whatever suits you, and your real friends will understand, and it stops people 'searching' for you. Be prepared to have many different names for the purpose of social media.

Social media can be a great tool. Just use it wisely. I haven't always and it has bitten me hard.

Change passwords on a regular basis. Although it's a

pain, it is Essentiall to keep your personal details, banking and emails secure.

Be prepared to be unpopular and for open criticism. You will develop a hard shell, and this will roll off you in time. Be prepared to cut people out of your life for life, no matter how close you once were.

Trust your gut. If someone or a situation makes you feel uncomfortable, tell them or the people you are with. If you are alone, talk to someone and tell them. You might come across as paranoid, but you will be surprised how many people are prepared to stick their necks out for a total stranger. I went out after dark one night on my own, and felt very uneasy. I told a work man working on the road, and he walked me to my destination and waited the few minutes and walked me home. Nothing happened, but who knows without his act of kindness whether something might have kicked off.

I have already said to talk to your friends and neighbours and if you have a photo, show them a photo of your abuser. My neighbours are some of my fiercest protectors. Retired but busy, they let me know if there are any 'strangers' hanging around, and have been known to 'confront' anyone who is hanging around. I do not recommend this at all. This puts them in the firing line, but I cannot stop them.

Do not have a routine. Change the way you drive or

walk to work and if you can, change the times too. Don't be frightened to ask for help.

If you don't have CCTV, try and get a Ring door-bell or the equivalent, so you don't have to open the door without knowing who is on the other side.

If you can, have an alarm installed, with panic buttons.

We installed a screen by the front door, so we can see who is at the door before we answer it, but it also allows me to check if there is anyone outside before I leave the house.

The police will arrange for contractors to fit anti-vandal paint to walls, plastic spikes on top of walls or fences, and alarms that fit onto windows.

I have a safe room in my house, that I can lock myself in. I have a mobile phone in there and I keep it charged for emergency calls only.

I have spent a lot of money on keeping me and my home secure that I will not put in here, as I don't want to advertise everything, but speak to the Crime Prevention Team in your area, and think of joining your Neighbour Watch scheme.

Don't use your mobile phone when you are out and about. Not only does it makes you a target for thieves but it also distracts you from your surroundings. You need to be aware, and you need to be contactable. I carry two mobile phones on different networks, both with an app called lone worker protection, that when activate makes a call to a Emergency Response Centre. Calls are monitored and recorded and they position you by your GPS co-ordinations. If you use your duress password or they hear the situation escalate, they involve the emergency services, and they seem to reach you far quicker than you dialling 999. In the sores case scenario, the calls are admissible in Court and there have been convictions as a result of compelling evidence.

Take care of yourself. I had a habit of drinking too much and it took a physiatrist to point out to me what I was doing to my body. This wasn't a sub-conscious thing. Years ago, I was out with a group from my former place of work and I hit my head when I had too much to drink. I didn't feel a thing until the next day.

So to my mind, if he was going to hurt me, I didn't want to feel it. Please don't get me wrong, I wasn't drunk all day every day, I worked and maintained a great life, but when things got too much for me, I would binge drink to block out how scared I always felt.

I am not tea total now, but I can enjoy one glass of wine, or one drink without the desire to blot my feelings out.

If you are meeting someone on a blind date, make people aware of where you are meeting and give a trusted friend all of the details. If you get to your date, excuse yourself for a bathroom break and text a prede-termined word which means the person you are meeting isn't who you were expecting, or something doesn't feel quite right. You should agree a plan beforehand, such as the friend turns up and joins you, or if you are really scared, they call the police.

Here we have a scheme called 'Ask for Angela', and I will help to get this rolled out throughout the country, the only problem is when a bar person's name really is Angela, so perhaps a name should be something else, like 'did you find my black trainer?' The scheme is simple, but indigenous.

Sign petitions from the charities to help change laws. We have a sex offenders register, why not a stalkers register, or a domestic abuse register. Sarah Law[1] and Claire's Law[2] were brought in because of tireless campaigning.

Eat well and exercise if you can, as this helps your mood and helps promote sleep. So does mediation, yoga and Pilates. I did self defence classes, learnt to run and did boot camp to improve my stamina, all high adrenaline pursuits to keep me safe, but it took a counsellor to point out that I also needed to learn to relax.

I read a book by Peter Collett, the Book of Tells and this was really helpful.

Read as many Survival Guides as you can lay your hands on. They all give good tips.

Use the 'Just Ask' website for legal advice. It is really affordable and I found a great barrister here.

If you have car or house insurance, make sure you have legal expenses cover. It costs about £6.00 a year and is worth every penny. They paid for my tribunal.

If you get invited out by a courier at work and you say no, but they keep asking, report it to your employer. They have a legal obligation to protect you and if you are made to feel uncomfortable, they should speak to the courier's employer.

If you are out, travel with others if you can. If you have to get a taxi alone, always take a photo with your mobile showing the badge number and make sure the driver see's you, and send it to a friend. If you get into a cab and there is no licence plate, get straight out.

Make a note of the registration and alert the police and council.

Don't walk home on your own, especially if you have had a drink. And don't let your friends either. Not only would you all feel awful if something happened to any of you, most of us would much prefer to sleep on a floor of a mates than risk being attacked or killed so stick together.

## DOMESTIC ABUSE

If you are the victim of domestic abuse, try and squirrel some money aside whenever you can, in an account your partner knows nothing about.

Make sure you do not receive statements at home, and hide your bank card in a safe place, whether that's at home, in the lining of an old show, at work, at a friends or a family member. If you regularly go for a coffee, try and switch and save the £3/4 a day instead. Cut back on anything other than the Essentiall. If you need to get out quick, it will help to have some money behind you.

Don't be embarrassed. Tell your employer if you feel able. Tell your closest friends. Tell your family if you can. There is an online course called The Freedom Course. Try and take it, it has helped many of my friends.

Tackling domestic abuse is a priority for many police

forces, with officers using new legislation and initiatives to better protect victims and those at risk.

Domestic abuse crime has increased nearly 12 per cent over the last year with domestic violence increasing over 18 percent in the same period.

To help tackle the issue, some police force's are currently piloting project PIPA (Preventing Intimate Partner Abuse), an early intervention approach whereby, if on first contact a domestic abuse incident meets the 'low harm' threshold, offenders are given a conditional caution and must agree to five sessions with programme PIPA to help them gain an insight into their behaviours and increase their motivation to make long-term changes.

The scheme has been successful in London and is now being piloted in other parts of the country, made possible by funding from the Office of the Police, Fire and Crime Commissioner. If successful, it will be adopted indefinitely.

So far, a total of 16 offenders have successfully completed the programme.

My local police force is also leading the way in its use of domestic violence protection orders (DVPOs). These provide extra protection to victims by enabling the police and magistrates' courts to put in place protective measures in the immediate aftermath of a domestic violence incident, where there is insufficient evidence to charge a perpetrator. They are designed to protect victims via bail conditions and 23 have been issued in the past month, the highest number in the East Midlands region.

Chief Inspector Julie Mead, who is the force lead for adult vulnerability, said "The increase in reports of domestic violence is encouraging as it proves victims are becoming more confident at reporting offences.

"Our use of DVPOs has been referenced as good practice in a recent HMICFRS (Her Majesty's Inspector of Constabulary and Fire Service) inspection report and we are also proud to be piloting project PIPA. Often victims of domestic abuse don't want their family to be torn apart – they want to stay with their partners and live safely with them. The project helps offenders understand the negative elements of their relationship so they can make changes after reflecting on the harm their behaviour is causing.

"We work closely with the courts, the Criminal Justice Unit and the CPS, with monthly meetings to review and revise all cases to make sure we're working effectively together. This force takes domestic abuse very seriously indeed and we have one of the highest arrest rates in the country for this type of crime."

Fiona Campbell, the Chief Executive Officer of Voice for Victims and Witnesses said "Voice knows how difficult it can be to speak out or seek help after you have been a victim of domestic abuse, but it is never too late to do so and Voice is here to assist you.

Voice is a free and confidential support service for anyone who has been a victim or witness of crime. The crime does not have to have been reported to the police and it doesn't matter when or where the crime was committed - Voice is here to offer support. Being a victim of crime can be life changing but you don't have to face this alone, whatever your situation Voice Specialist Caseworkers are here to assist you, you can contact us on 0300 303 1965 or at www.voicenorthants.org."

Police, Fire and Crime Commissioner Stephen Mold said "I was pleased to be able to bring Project PIPA to the locality as it is based on the best evidence of what works to make the perpetrators of domestic abuse understand the impact of their behaviour on their partner and children and to stop the abuse. It also ensures the victim's wishes are at the heart of the process, as they have to agree to the offender taking part in the project. We are still very early on in the pilot scheme, but the offenders will be tracked over a period of two years to measure Project PIPA's effectiveness in stopping people who have admitted abuse from offending again.

"I am confident that this groundbreaking approach will be a real change with better outcomes for victims and I thank my team and the police officers involved who have worked hard to bring this to fruition."

1
SARAH'S LAW, OR THE CHILD SEX OFFENDER DISCLOSURE SCHEME ALLOWS PARENTS, CARERS AND GUARDIANS TO ASK THE POLICE TO TELL THEM IF SOMEONE HAS A CRIMINAL RECORD FOR CHILD SEXUAL OFFENCES.

THE SCHEME IS FOR ANY MEMBER OF THE PUBLIC WHO WANTS TO FIND OUT IF AN INDIVIDUAL IN CONTACT WITH A CHILD HAS A RECORD OF CHILD SEXUAL OFFENCES.

IF POLICE CHECKS SHOW THE INDIVIDUAL HAS A RECORD FOR CHILD SEXUAL OFFENCES, OR OTHER OFFENCES THAT MIGHT PUT THE CHILD AT RISK, THE POLICE WILL CONSIDER SHARING THIS INFORMATION. THE POLICE WILL ONLY CONSIDER TELLING THE PERSON BEST PLACED TO PROTECT THE CHILD — USUALLY A PARENT, CARER OR GUARDIAN — IF THE PERSON BEING CHECKED HAS A RECORD OF CHILD SEXUAL OFFENCES OR OTHER OFFENCES THAT INDICATE THEY MAY POSE A RISK TO A CHILD. THE POLICE WILL DISCLOSE INFORMATION ONLY IF IT IS LAWFUL, NECESSARY AND PROPORTIONATE TO DO SO IN THE INTERESTS OF PROTECTING THE CHILD, OR CHILDREN, FROM HARM.

2
CLARE'S LAW: MAKE A DOMESTIC VIOLENCE DISCLOSURE SCHEME (DVDS) APPLICATION IF SOMEONE IS IN DANGER OR AT RISK

IF YOU OR SOMEONE YOU KNOW IS BEING ABUSED YOU CAN TELL US ABOUT THIS, EITHER BY CALLING 101 OR ONLINE. IF YOU'RE DEAF OR HARD OF HEARING, USE OUR TEXTPHONE SERVICE ON 18001 101.

IF THERE'S AN IMMEDIATE RISK TO SOMEONE'S SAFETY, PLEASE CALL 999. IF YOU'RE DEAF OR HARD OF HEARING, USE OUR TEXTPHONE SERVICE 18000 OR

TEXT US ON 999 IF YOU'VE PRE-REGISTERED WITH THE EMERGENCY SMS SERVICE.

THIS FORM ISN'T FOR REPORTING DOMESTIC ABUSE. IF YOU NEED TO DO THAT, PLEASE GO HERE.

**PLEASE NOTE:** *THE DOMESTIC VIOLENCE DISCLOSURE SCHEME (DVDS) DOESN'T REPLACE CRIMINAL RECORDS BUREAU (CRB) CHECKS, SUBJECT ACCESS OR FREEDOM OF INFORMATION (FOI) REQUESTS AND THE NEW DISCLOSURE AND BARRING SERVICE.*

# AFTERWORD
## RELEVANT CONTACT DETAILS

**Paladin National Stalking Advocacy Service**

Telephone 0207 840 8960

Paladinservice.co.uk

Email info@paladinservice.co.uk

**The Suzy Lamplugh Trust**

Telephone 0207 091 0014

http://suzylamplugh.org

info@suzylamplugh.org

**Victims Support**

Telephone 0845 3030900

http://www.victimssupport.org.uk

## Woman's Aid

Telephone 0808 2000 247 Free-phone 24-hour National Domestic Violence Helpline

http://www.refuge.org.uk

## National Centre for Domestic Violence

0844 8044 999

www.NCDV.org.uk

text NCDV to 60777 and they will call back

## Protection Against Stalking

www.protectionagainststalking.org

## Network for Surviving Stalking

https://www.scaredofsomeone.org/

## Crown Prosecution Services

http://cps.gov.uk/legal/s

## ACKNOWLEDGMENTS

I want to thank from the bottom of my heart those who supported me, who didn't advise me to 'let it go', who knew that for my own peace of mind, I had to explore all the avenues available to me, even when many were a waste of time and energy.

I can't name you all personally although I have thanked you all over the years. And most of all I have to thank my beloved for letting me deal with the situation my way. I know the level of restraint I asked for was an enormous effort on your part, but although it was frustrating he ended up with the conviction.

You did not.

## ABOUT THE AUTHOR

Anne B Suza is an emerging author with this, Murder in Slow Motion, her debut novel.

The paperback is due for release in early 2020.

Anne remains a stance supporter of actions against stalking and harassment of any kind.

Printed in Poland
by Amazon Fulfillment
Poland Sp. z o.o., Wrocław

53713964R00074

# North Fylde

## IN OLD PHOTOGRAPHS

C000138274

Singleton Mill, *c.* 1898.

# North Fylde

## IN OLD PHOTOGRAPHS

### Collected by
### CATHERINE ROTHWELL

Alan Sutton Publishing Limited
Phoenix Mill · Far Thrupp · Stroud
Gloucestershire

First Published 1992

Copyright © Catherine Rothwell, 1992

Front Cover Illustration:
Ferry Dock, Fleetwood, early this century.

This book is dedicated to
Eleanor, James and Patrick

British Library Cataloguing
in Publication Data

Rothwell, Catherine
North Fylde in Old Photographs
I. Title
942. 766

ISBN 0-7509-0239-6

Typset in 9/10 Sabon
Typesetting and origination by
Alan Sutton Publishing Limited.
Printed and bound by
WBC, Bridgend, Mid Glam.

Fleetwood lifeboatmen, 1931: Dick Abram, 'Coosh' Wright, Jim Leadbetter, Dick Wright, Sid Hill, Harry Bond, Jeff Wright (on cannon), Bill Houston.

# *Contents*

Introduction     6

1.   Poulton-le-Fylde     9

2.   Bispham, Thornton, Cleveleys     53

3.   Fleetwood     83

4.   Across the River     133

Acknowledgements     160

# *Introduction*

When the tribes of the Segantii roved and ranged year round, from the Fells of Bowland to the Rossall coastal strip and Highfurlong (the skeleton of a hunted glacial elk with barbed bone darts was discovered in 1971), and, later, when ancient Amounderness became known as Fylde its confines were not clearly drawn. Shrouded in mists, a land of bogs and meres, 'a county within a county', the Fylde proved to be a haven for the pursued and persecuted. Gentlemen farmers drained the mosslands, transforming them into the Cornfield of Lancashire, and the Fylde became a prestigious place in which to live, so that many who were not entitled to do so claimed to dwell within its borders.

Such an area was bound to be opened up with the coming of railways, steamships, motor charabancs and the electric tramroad. Sea, country, hills, river, a rolling plain for easy access; the entrepreneurs rubbed their hands, each 'setting to' in his own way – Dr Cocker, Elijah Hargreaves, Margaret Parkinson, T.G. Lumb, Fleetwood Estate Company, Gynn Estate Company, Benjamin C. Sykes, and so on. Bricklayers became building contractors overnight. Cheap trips on the railway, advertisements, and time-tables flooded the mill towns, beckoning visitors for stays in the Fylde with its 'charming scenery, lovely country walks, glorious sunsets, the bounding main'.

In the leisurely days of 1908, whisked along the coast on a comfortable Fleetwood Tramroad Company car, the tripper was introduced to Bispham, 'the pretty village with the historic church'. (When harvests failed in 'Pea Soup Year' the villagers' staple diet was a cargo of peas washed up from a wreck.) And to Norbreck, 'a rising resort which the YMCA have chosen for camp'. Proudly pointed out also was Cleveleys Hydropathic Hotel, as was Cleveleys Park and its 'artistic dwellings'. Next came Rossall Hall, home of the Northern School for the Sons of Gentlemen and Clergy, formerly the residence of Sir Peter Hesketh Fleetwood, the sad baronet friend of Queen Victoria, who had sunk almost his entire fortune into establishing a port and fashionable holiday resort, Fleetwood-on-Wyre.

Early this century the gigantic North American Grain Elevator, which showed 1882 on its gable end in white tile numerals so large they could be discerned from the foothills of North Fylde, dominated a seaport receiving ships from all over the world. Trawler-spotting and the extensive dock were a great tourist draw. Returning home with a 2s. 6d. parcel of fresh Fleetwood fish, hearing the story of Mr Blezard, who owned *Orphesia* FD 119, known as 'the toffee boat' because supplies of toffee were sent aboard for the crew (Mr Blezard also owned a sweet factory) – all this must have added lustre to the day.

A walk along the stone quay, eyeing the Belfast, Isle of Man, Barrow and Morecambe boats, roused appetites. What better than to call in at Durrant's London Dining Rooms opposite the fine railway station, whose interior resembled nothing less than a well-kept conservatory!

'You must board one of the jaunty little steamers crossing the Wyre every few minutes,' said one guide book. At long last Knot End had become the terminus for the railway from Garstang, thus opening up still further outposts of North Fylde.

And there was choice in those golden summers, with change from a guinea still in one's pocket at the end of the day. Bonney's Livery Stables in central Blackpool had started to run a coach tour: 'As we wend our way, the guard makes the vicinity ring with his merry tootling of the post horn, calling to mind the good old coaching days.'

The first extensive view of North Fylde was gained at Hoo Hill, from where a stretch of rich pasture, dotted with the dwellings of yeomen farmers, windmills and white thatched cottages spread for miles.

The driver pulled up at 'the ancient metropolis of Poulton', outside the Black Bull with its own brewhouse on the site of the earliest well in the village. Its carved-oak sign was so large and sturdy that the innkeeper, Jabez Catterall, could sit astride it and did so on Festival Days, the wooden bull draped with flags and bunting. Less than a century before, in a Newcastle tract, the market town had been described as 'Poolton in the Foil in the *wild* parts of Lancashire'.

Built of iron and dating from 1864, Shard Bridge was summed up as 'quaint, 325 yards long, costing £13,000'. Time has proved that it paid for itself. An ancient ford ran close by, one of six over the river, which on market days had been so congested that wagons often overturned as they jostled for position.

At this point the traveller caught his first glimpse of the River Wyre, wide-spreading over sea holly and thrift if the tide was in. A pleasant day could be spent at the ancient ports of Wardleys and Skippool from where the Six Sisters had sailed with emigrants for the New World. 'Bowling Green, boating, enjoyable fishing in the Wyre' were enticements, but most chose to canter on down country lanes abounding with flowers, the heavy scent of hawthorn hedges borne on the breeze, winding lanes with S-bends and thick-set living boundaries filled with bird song. The smell of peat fuel floated from white-sided, cobble-stoned, thatched cottages, their orchards 'boughed' to the ground with blossom or fruit and here and there a TEA sign, further enticement with home-produced eggs, butter, ham, strawberries, cream and home-made bread and scones on the menu.

'The garden village of the Fylde', Stalmine, with its grange (peaches grew on walls heated with charcoal), had the Pack Horse Hotel and some beautiful rose gardens. Then it was on to Preesall Park's whitewashed windmill, the children still chewing Mrs Swarbrick's Wardleys Toffee washed down with Hodgkinson's mineral water, usually ginger beer. They might catch sight of Mr Bisbrown, corn miller, white with flour.

Perhaps father fancied a ride on the Garstang and Knott End Railway, for there were stations at Pilling, Preesall and Stakepool. After the grass-grown track of the last five miles had finally been completed ('it is called Knott End', wrote the exasperated local cleric, the Revd J. Banister, 'because it does not end.') Mr G. Erroll Worthington, general manager of the railway, would be on hand to welcome holidaymakers in Wakes Weeks or on Bank Holidays. Messrs Manning and Wardle of Leeds had specially built 'new engines of a modern type' with eight new carriages capable of carrying fifty persons and similar to those running on the London Underground. These last were supplied by the Birmingham Waggon Company and, though they ran so slowly that some jokers suggested you could get out and pick flowers along the way, they were grand indeed and what is more they ran on time owing to 'telephonic communication between stations'.

With such facilities, easy access was to be had to sixteenth-century Parrox Hall, the salt mines of which produced a much-prized, brilliantly white and flocculent salt (locally it was spread to sweeten old pastures, but it was also shipped to India); Pilling, 'loveliest village of the plain', akin to sweet Auburn; and the celebrated Gull Moss, a part of North Fylde which resisted all efforts of drainage. To visit the last-mentioned, a permit was required from the appropriately named owner, Colonel Bird. Over the treacherous bog-land the wary tripper followed his guide, to be rewarded with the wonderful sight of thousands of white seagulls wheeling on the wind or upon nests so thickly clustered that it was impossible to walk amongst them. Edwin Waugh, Lancashire dialect poet, had visited when he stayed at Norbreck. Mine host at the nearest hotel to Gull Island was Roger Ireton of the Elletson's Arms. At some time during the outing you might, if you were lucky, see Joseph Cumpstey, the oldest town crier in Lancashire, who lived at Churchtown.

Times were changing, for Mr R.W. Lang, who advertised as 'hot water and sanitary plumber', had just installed a bicycle and motor department where Dunlop tyres, and Pratt's and Shell Motor Spirit were for sale.

Sooner or later you would be sure to return to see that giant tower, Marsh Hill, built by Bold Fleetwood Hesketh at Thornton-le-Fylde where ploughing matches were held and the shopkeepers advertised in rhyme:

> This is a shop for a pot and a pan,
> A place for a jug and a kettle,
> But if there's nothing you want to buy
> Please bring us something to fettle.

The travelling tinkers were also prospering and settling down!

As for entertainment in North Fylde, besides magic lantern shows, and pierrots and bands, minstrels were provided by Percy Clifton on the foreshore and on the streets of Fleetwood District in the summer season of 1900, a year when the Pleasure Boat Company was so busy that it negotiated for extra landing-stage facilities. In the following year came popular Solly's Concert Party on the sands. Emmie Ford, appearing on tour at the Queen's Theatre, wrote home that she had seen this lively show ('The Kissing Duet' brought the house down) and that next week she would move on to the Palace at Oldbury, near Birmingham.

And the happy tripper of those days would be sure to hear about North Fylde characters, some of them octogenarians and centenarians, who still did a day's work: Old Doilee, Dusty Miller, Red Sal, Hungry Mitchell, 'Owd' England, and Joseph Gornall, a quality cheese-maker whose invention sold from 1892 to 1919.

Generations of visitors have come to North Fylde – and still they come. In this collection of evocative photographs I have included personal anecdote to capture atmosphere and convey the spirit of the age. Like water from a spring, this has a flavour and freshness of its own.

Catherine Rothwell

# SECTION ONE
# Poulton-le-Fylde

Thatched cottages in Little Poulton Lane dating from the seventeenth century.

Parkinson and Tomlinson, millers and corn dealers, are listed in an 1892 directory as having a business in Banks Street, later known as Chapel Street. This photograph may be by Maynard Tomlinson, a local photographer. The corn mill was pulled down in the 1960s. Notice the horse wearing blinkers and the millers, always white with flour, unlike the village chimney sweep who was black from soot.

Staining Mill. This engraving exemplifies rural Fylde, once known as Windmill Land or the Cornfield of Lancashire. As a special treat on 19 October 1909, Class 1 at the National School was allowed to 'watch from Staining Hill the aeroplane flying'. These were the early days of experimental, sustained flight.

Premises of Poulton blacksmith Hugh Simmons, 1890–1909, which were owned by his family until the 1950s. Hugh won prizes for shoeing horses at competitions from Barrow-in-Furness to continental Europe. On festival days floats were elaborately decorated, the blacksmiths taking on board a horse, anvil and plenty of horse shoes.

Corner House, dating from the eighteenth century, which still survives, although much changed. The thatched cottage has gone. May Day dancing and the crowning of a May King and Queen were held on this part of The Green. Dancing went on into the night, some of the farmers showing skill and staying power.

Queen's Square, Poulton, early this century, under snow. The lamp would nowadays be a collector's item. In this area stood the elegant town house of Misses Ethel and Edith Viener, who were keen leaders of Poulton girl guides and boy scouts. One of the sisters launched a lifeboat.

Miss Hull, daughter of the Revd John Hull, vicar of St Chad's church, in the 1860s. The clergy included the curate, the Revd Robert Bowness, whose son, Dr Robert H. Bowness, was medical officer for the Fylde Union. This is the oldest photograph in the book.

Country lane, Hardhorn, c. 1900. The wooden building on the right sold home-made lemonade, sarsaparilla, ginger beer and nettle drink. Edward Jolly, joiner and builder, and Richard Bennett, boot and shoe maker, had premises not far away. Baines Endowed School, restored in 1881, was also in the vicinity.

The Railway and Station Hotel, run by Samuel Castle in the 1900s, stood alongside the original Poulton railway station on the Preston and Wyre line. Other Poulton inns were the King's Arms, Black Bull, Bay Horse, Ship, Wheatsheaf and Sportsman's, all of which were busy on market days serving 'The Metropolis of the Fylde'.

Thatched cottages in Breck Road, *c.* 1900. These were sketched in pen and ink in 1860 by J.W. Green, a Fleetwood artist who was also well known for his paintings of steam trawlers. Similar cottages, 300 years old, once lined Church Street and Ball Street, the Thatched House inn being part of the scene.

Poulton Market Square in the days of the wagonette. It is full of history: stocks, market cross, the Bull Hotel with sign and lamp, Emma Whitton's grocers shop on the left and the Lancaster Banking Company, open Mondays and Tuesdays, 10.30 a.m.–2.30 p.m. The very early cobblestones, which had given Poulton the name 'town of petrified kidneys', have been replaced by setts.

'Perfection in Flake Tobacco.' The advertisement is on the gable end of Richards' ironmongers shop, No. 2 Market Place, the oldest agricultural business premises in the Fylde. Farmers and labourers came here to buy tedders, rakes, pitchforks, wheelbarrows, harrows, ploughs, drills and billhooks.

Medieval Tithe Barn, where corn was threshed with hand flails. A tithe or tenth, along with other produce, went to the lord of the manor. Poulton was the poorer for losing this building, shown on the right with the tower of St Chad's church above it.

Sheaf Street. An artist's impression showing an agricultural worker carrying a pitchfork, with a child beside him. On the left is the eighteenth-century house of clockmaker Mr Lomas. Poulton retained its old-world atmosphere into the 1900s and was a paradise for artists. I.H. Blakeley sketched Tithebarn Street and its 1770s cottages built of clay, cobbles, straw and tree trunks.

Horses outside the Bay Horse Inn, licensee W.H. Cooper. Horse fairs were held regularly in the Market Square. Robert S. Tyler and Robert Miller, horse dealers, lived on The Green and saddler Richard Parkinson in Market Place. G. Dalton on Breck Road was the last saddler in Poulton.

Gleaming shire horse and corduroy-clad labourer employed by Mr Dagger, *c.* 1910, stand outside Compley Farm, the area where Teanley Night bonfire customs were once held annually. Henry Martindale was at Butler Farm, William Rossall at Oldfield Carr and Thomas Clarkson at Angel Holme, where boat-building was carried on during the reign of Elizabeth I.

Chrysanthemum Show Committee at Sheaf Street School, Hardhorn Road, *c.* 1924. Back row, from left to right: Percy Wilkinson, J. Barnes, Smalley, Sanderson, Ashton, Hodgson, -?-, -?-, Plant, Sanderson, -?-, R. Simmons, Holland, Rob. Balderstone. Front row: Coupe, Potter, the Revd Mr Mellor, R. Balderstone Jnr, Mrs Sharples, Mr Sharples, Warbreck, the Revd Mr Pope, R. Minshull, H. Dutton. This popular flower show is still held every autumn in Poulton-le-Fylde, a town that has made a feature of electing committees to organize important events. To prepare for Queen Victoria's Jubilees, prominent names such as Bowness, Henderson, Thornber, Harrison featured on the lists, and months of preparation went into the processions in which marched such organizations as the Mechanics, the Order of Buffaloes, Freemasons, Oddfellows, Clergy, and the Tontine Society.

A North Fylde farmer and his dog, *c.* 1908. The view across Queen's Square to Sheaf Street, which got its name from the Wheatsheaf Inn where farmers gathered, indicates it is not market day. 'Wiseacres' weather wisdom was still acceptable in this predominantly farming community. 'If Candlemas Day be fair and clear there will be two winters in one year.' Newspapers recorded that March 1908 was the driest on record.

This gentleman farmer, who hailed from Yorkshire, may have served on Poulton Urban District Council under its first chairman, W. Hodgson of The Sycamores. Hodgson School commemorates this man, who did so much for education. Poulton was governed by its UDC from 1900 to 1974. Members of the 1924 council included Robert Parkinson, John Balderstone and Dr W. Riddle.

Sheaf Street School, on the right with an old street lamp outside, was opened in 1830, later becoming the Church of England School. Logbook entries show low attendance at haytime and harvest in 1881, and on 28 January 1910 when snow was so deep that only 12 children out of 112 attended.

The Tithe Barn was used for many purposes, including play performances. Tickets, available from the Golden Ball or Mr Thompson, printer, cost one or two shillings, with half price after 8 p.m. An 1882 poster advertised *Pizarro or the Spaniard in Peru*. These early posters offer plants.

The Merry Milkmaids of Staining. On the right near the teacher is Mary Webster, whose father had a milk round in Staining. Children helped on the farm at an early age, the girls usually in the dairy, making cheese and butter. Alice Jane Livesey, born in February 1897, remembered earning 3s. 6d. per month for helping a Carleton farmer with the milk.

Richard Webster's milk float did the rounds in the 1920s, delivering twice a day, after morning and evening milking. Milk churns, kits (milk pails) with different-sized measures, and ladles were regularly scalded, the kits being strapped on the float. Besides the farmers, there were individual cowkeepers like Margaret Cartmell and John Lawrenson.

Carleton Gala. Beyond the wrought-iron arch was the turnstile leading into Castle Gardens, which had an aviary and specialized in strawberry and cream teas at gala time. 'Up all night making paper roses for Archway on Castle Gardens,' was one of Alice Penswick's memories.

Poulton Road early this century. Across from the group of children is Kilshaw's Farm and the wheelwrights shop. Beyond Four Lane Ends was 'Jonty' Greenwood's, which sold oatcakes, bread and teacakes. Bowler's wooden hut sold treacle dabs, Fry's chocolate bars, penny bottles of pop and ginger beer – all clearly remembered by Alice Jane Livesey.

J. Parkinson's general store and post office, Carleton. This seventeenth-century thatched dwelling was in the family for several generations. Treacle sold loose in a jug, oatmeal, flour, butter and lard were among the best-selling commodities, but other goods sold included flypapers, donkey stones, paraffin and firelighters. Cows were kept in the orchard behind the shop.

Carleton Garage, which is still the site of a filling station, must have raised eyebrows when it set up in business opposite the Castle Hotel, which advertised its 'pleasure grounds and accommodation for visitors'. The smithy, not far away on Poulton Road, was still busy shoeing horses, serving thirty-two farms in Carleton. One of the few vehicles to be seen was the dog cart of Florrie Greenhalgh, whose family owned the Ladies' Bowling Club. The coming of the petrol engine was to change all that.

Sheaf Street National School, now Poulton Church of England School. The schoolmistress in this group, Miss A.J. Tebay, occasionally helped out at the cobblestone-walled school at Carleton. Gardening was taught and school records show that children were taken for 'nature walks to see the blossom'. During the First World War, in autumn 1918, the top class collected over 2 cwt of blackberries. These and fresh eggs were sent to wounded soldiers cared for in a large house turned into the auxiliary hospital.

The people of Daisy Colony, standing outside Higham House, were a group of people who worked together on the land. The Wilsons lived at Higham Farm nearby, and there was a Higham Cottage, but all these buildings were sacrificed when a new road and housing estate were built. The card is postmarked August 1905.

Shakespeare's *Henry VIII* is acted by a group of girls from Miss Cryer's private school on the Breck. Around the turn of the century the four Cryer sisters at Breck Villa were headed by Mary and Clara. The school closed down between the wars, as did a number of other private schools in Poulton.

This motor crash occurred in quiet Poulton in June 1933. One can imagine the wiseacres gathering and saying 'Told you so.' In the background on the left is the Methodist chapel, now demolished. Some years earlier Walker's shop had been called Peg's Sweet Shop and appears on an older photograph of the Higher Green area.

The Corner Shop on Chapel Street, 1900. The premises of Thompson's, Provision Dealers, with long-gowned ladies outside, are typical of the small trader. Although Poulton was considered a village at the beginning of the century, it had five butchers and five tailors. Joseph Rawcliffe was a butcher in Church Street, followed ten years later by James Roskell. Joseph Cowell retired in 1931 after being the postman for fifty years. On his rounds he would call at such shops as Maggie Swarbrick's, which sold only parched peas, Lizzie Hart's dairy, Emma Ellison's chip shop, Clegg's the clogger, Whitton's, and Lawrenson's stationer. From 1695 to 1851 window tax was in force, and it was common to block up windows to avoid this as in this photograph. Land extending the full length of Vicarage Lane and right across to the old thatched cottages in Lower Green was glebe land belonging to the Church.

The River Wyre inn, Poulton-le-Fylde, is thought to be the only inn named after a river. Built in 1896, it overlooks Skippool Creek, where Skipton Brook joins the River Wyre. On gala days in the early 1900s the morris dancers finished here, where they were given glasses of lemonade.

Carleton Morris Dancers in their uniforms of white dresses and green sashes. Practice was in the Memorial Hall, which commemorated soldiers who died in the First World War. The maypole dancers were trained by Miss Perkins, the maypole having been made at a joiners shop on Blackpool Road that later became a butchers premises.

Morris dancers and their trainer in Sheaf Street, now Hardhorn Road. The photograph shows a happy occasion in the 1920s: Union Jacks and bunting in the background suggest a royal occasion or a Poulton Festival celebration.

A wedding day at the Methodist chapel, *c.* 1926, with a white-ribboned car awaiting the bride and groom. Wesleyan Methodism came to the Fylde in about 1810 when the pioneers had to battle against prejudice and ill treatment to become established. Eleven members adopted the faith in Poulton and missionary Moses Holden wrote: 'I opened the whole of the Fylde county and formed classes in different villages.' Their first simple chapel was in use by 1810, half a century before this stronger chapel, which gave Chapel Street its name. A larger building was erected on Queensway and the chapel in this photograph razed in 1965 and replaced by a dry cleaners and bank.

Police and Poulton Brass Band, established 1875. This postcard would appear to show the local council being escorted to church on their special Sunday some time in the early 1900s. The church chosen would be that attended by the leader of the council. The photograph shows how narrow Ball Street was.

Clarkson and Bennett's butchers shop and Hunter's Tea Store in the early 1900s. Because of demand, shop fronts were appearing on town houses, whose elegant proportions, with their quoins and dripstones, are clearly shown.

The Prince of Wales visited Poulton in 1927 during a tour of the Fylde. He is seen outside Mayor's pork butchers at Nos 12–14 Market Place before reviewing veteran ex-service-men. Mayor's was one of the town's oldest businesses listed in street directories of the 1920s.

Premises of G. Richardson, architect, who practised in the Fylde in the 1920s. The newspaper delivery boy seen here would have shouted the news headlines while running through the streets with a poster fixed to his waist. The arched entry on the right once led to notorious Potts Alley with its rowdy seamen's lodging houses.

Mr Tom Darville had a shop in Poulton but also took his produce around the streets on this handcart. Fruit, greengrocery, poultry and rabbits were for sale. Tom always wore a sacking apron and cried his wares: 'Five pounds of potatoes and a rabbit, sixpence.'

Hayfield Avenue was once called Holly Street, where in 1924 Agnes Cowrie was grocer. The travelling photographer would look for farms and street scenes and it was popular to be photographed outside one's house. The photograph would then be made into a greetings card to send at Christmas or Easter.

Highfield House with its large garden in the 1920s, when folding deck chairs became popular and synonymous with sun bathing. One young man lodging in Holly Street never remembered actually sitting in one but he did spend much time removing and replacing deck chair canvas for his landlady. Deck chairs of chenille or tapestry with canopies were even greater luxuries.

Poulton Gala procession winds down Higher Green to Lower Green in the 1920s. The horses and floats depict town life. From the 1900s the Misses Tebay were the main organizers, it being convenient to work from Sheaf Street School as the scholars were involved. Starting as Poulton Club Day, it became the high spot of the year. Clergy, councillors, Oddfellows, bands, morris dancers, petal strewers, scouts and guides walked around the town, the 'swells' and the Festival Queen in landaus.

St Chad's church tower, built in the reign of Charles I, was photographed before new lamps appeared and gravestones were removed in the 1970s. A 900-year-old foundation, the sandstone church was taken down in August 1751 to be rebuilt when the Revd Robert Loxham was vicar. During that time services had to be held in the Tithe Barn and baptisms in cottages. Money to rebuild the church was said to have been squandered by farmers. The poor of the parish were so indignant at the expense that Mr Welsh of Marton refused to contribute, writing a poem to that effect.

The arms of the Rigby family were originally on their town house situated opposite the stocks where the National Westminster Bank now stands. This photograph shows their present position. Behind, in the lee of the tower, is the eighteenth-century font, discovered in the garden of the old vicarage.

A Lomas clock, perhaps the only one still surviving in Poulton. Samuel and Richard Lomas, father and son, made grandfather clocks in the eighteenth century. They lived at what is now No. 16 Hardhorn Road. The churchwarden's accounts from that century refer to 'payment, Mr Lomas, for mending clock'.

Ball Street, Poulton, 1910. This photograph was among those commissioned when buildings surrounding the church were under a demolition order. Mr R.N. Lord, local 'likeness taker', was given the task of making a record. In 1842 Poulton Petty Sessions were held in the Golden Ball, which still stands, but the row of old houses opposite, including a fish and chip shop and the premises of Mr J.P. Dobson, joiner and builder, had to go. Large hoardings at the end of this terrace used to advertise Blackpool shows.

Poulton War Memorial in Queen's Square has been removed to Market Square since the head boy of Baines's Grammar School laid this wreath on 11 November 1932. Clergy are the Congregational minister and the vicar of St Chad's, the Revd Mr Mellor. The Greek frieze above what was once Parkinson's Corn Millers bakers shop, run by Robert Parkinson Jnr, is a reminder of the 'Cornfield of Amounderness', that fertile Fylde plain, and the presence of many windmills to grind the flour. The premises are now occupied by the Furness Building Society.

Floral procession to St Chad's church, July 1910. Led by Poulton Brass Band, the girls, dressed in white, carry local flowers. At the funeral of Thomas Clegg, a Carleton School trustee, all the schoolchildren walked behind the coffin from Carleton to Poulton. By 1884 there were 92 scholars under one teacher, Isabella Holmes.

Georgian town houses. Opposite the ancient Tithe Barn, the mark of a medieval market town, there were thatched cottages cheek by jowl with three-storey town houses. On the left are houses that were the homes of Doctor Bowness, John Braid his coachman (the village tooth puller) and Alexander Moore. They were demolished in the 1960s.

The County Court, later the public library, at the corner of Queen's Square and Sheaf Street. The court's jurisdiction covered Poulton, Bispham, Kirkham, Lytham, Preesall and Stalmine. Paul Thornber was Clerk to the Magistrates, the best known of whom was Giles Thornber, who died 21 April 1860, aged 85.

The Market Place, with stocks, cross, fish stones, whipping post and the lamp erected to commemorate Queen Victoria's Jubilee. In 1891 the town had a population of 1,412 and a rateable value of £8,774. It was here that the important trade of North Fylde was done.

Breck Road, 1924. Mr Anderson's Vulcan lorry and the Blackpool omnibus CK 4286 stand opposite A.E. Lloyd's dentists premises and the chemists shop. A poster advertises *Ship from Shanghai*, showing at Poulton Picture House in Vicarage Road. What could be termed another veteran is the telephone kiosk near the Conservative Club, which was the Ship Inn in the days when Poulton was a port.

On the Breck in the 1920s a solitary car, having passed Judge Parry's house, makes its way towards Breck Lodge (built 1810), now a haven for the elderly. In Little Poulton Lane, once a hamlet of thatched cruck-built cottages, Little Poulton Hall (built 1695) and Old Farm (built 1723), initialled 'P.H.C.', still stand.

A Ribble double-decker bus at the bottom of Breck Road heads for Thornton-le-Fylde in the 1930s when all traffic passed through The Square. It follows part of a time-honoured route taken by the stage coaches. On the left is Moorland Road, area of 'the great moor land' marked on old maps. Down this road in the 1900s came wagonettes for that 'New Drive to the magnificent Country Mansion, The Manor'.

Thornfield Holiday Camp, Staining, was established to attract town dwellers to the Fylde countryside in the 1920s and 1930s. In the background is Singleton Mill. Coast, countryside and river amenities have since brought caravan sites to Windy Harbour and Cartford Bridge.

The River Wyre, Great Eccleston, 1920. This area near Poulton is vulnerable to flooding. The last severe flood was on 11 November 1977, when Fylde coastal towns were inundated and high tidal river conditions were created inland.

Poulton Festival float, 1929. The coal wagon carrying a display depicting village life has won a prize. Swags, drapes, paper flowers and a Wendy House with children in smocks and mob caps have persuaded the judges. This was an exciting day for all including Dobbin the horse with his plaited, beribboned tail and shining brasses.

Twenty Steps, a tall, four-storey town house sited opposite the Bay Horse Inn, which is now the Old Town Hall public house. It towered above Church Street and by the 1800s had been turned into tenement dwellings. It was demolished in 1910.

Miss Alice Milner, beauty queen, was employed as a mannequin by Windsor Woollies, a Poulton firm noted for quality. Alice, a Thornton girl, attended the Wignall Memorial Methodist church, where she later married Gordon Lancaster. Here she is seen modelling Jacquard Windsor water woollies, *c.* 1930.

Sir Peter Hesketh Fleetwood appears with his daughter, Anna Maria, painted by Margaret Carpenter in 1837. Not many years later this surviving child of his first marriage, aged 11, died of consumption, a disease that had proved a scourge to his family. The family vault at St Chad's church, of which Sir Peter was patron, contains Anna Maria's embalmed body.

Illawalla, home of Vesta Tilley, in the 1920s. Here, with her husband, Sir Walter de Frece, the vaudeville artiste and male impersonator entertained a galaxy of stage stars. When the Waits came at Christmas they were invited into the luxury bungalow to be rewarded with mince pies and half crowns. The empty building is now under threat of demolition.

An *Illustrated London News* engraving from a newspaper found in Poulton shows 'Paris fashions for November 1863', including 'bonnets, soft and rich in appearance, a series in amethyst coloured velvet.' 1. Promenade dress for a young lady, 2. Walking dress, and 3. Home toilet. The materials sound wonderful – grey mohair, green moire, velvet, lace, violet silk. Fashionable ladies changed their outfits three times a day.

Demolition in the 1960s, when the heart of the old village was swept away, including Butler's Farm and Carr's Cottage, the thatched dwelling where Henry Hargreave lived in 1892. Teanlowe Shopping Centre was built, a reminder of Teanley Night, when villagers stood in a circle holding blazing bundles of straw on pitchforks to guide lost souls to heaven – hence the name Purgatory Field.

An old grindstone, 2 ft in diameter and overgrown by a sycamore tree, was found on the site of Whiteside's Farm at the end of Taylor's Lane, now Arundel Drive, by Matthew Conefery, site foreman for Norwest Housing. In 1973 the Department of the Environment had released 60.97 acres of land for residential development.

Catterall and Swarbrick's horse and cart, loaded with workmen, stands at the Castle Gardens Inn, Carleton. Brewers of ale and porter, 'C. and S.' had premises at the Queen's Brewery, Queen's Square, Poulton, and at Newton. In spring and summer, hundreds of wagonette trips brought visitors from Blackpool to look over Captain Fitzroy's Pleasure Gardens.

The morris dancers of Staining, c. 1900. The dancers are assembled in Mill Lane, with Joseph Crampton's windmill in the background, and represent an earlier stage of the dance. Centuries-old morris featured frilled bonnets, black stockings, white dresses and flower garlands symbolizing May.

'A Friend in Need' is passing a glass of ale to the chimney sweep in the stocks, *c.* 1900. This was a posed photograph sold to visitors. The stocks have been knocked down by passing traffic many times but visitors today still sit in the stocks to be photographed.

Councillor H. Ashworth chairs the last meeting of Poulton Urban District Council on 24 May 1973, the year before local government reorganization included Poulton in the area of Wyre Borough Council. Mr J. Whittingslow, Clerk of the Council, is on the left and Councillor J.E. Gorst on the right. Previously, meetings had taken place in the Town Hall, Church Street.

# Bispham, Thornton, Cleveleys

The tide comes in at Cleveleys.

Old Bispham village, an artist's impression of particular value as all has now changed. Apart from a small newsagents shop, not one building of any antiquity remains. In February 1937 some of the oldest cottages in Bispham were bulldozed for a road-widening scheme. The 300-year-old cobble-stone cottages were remembered by Mr J. Parkinson of All Hallows Road. One was kept as the Tuck Shop by Jimmy and Nibby Hornby, who allowed the lads of the village to play cards there. Three shops provided all requirements, including that popular commodity, black treacle. Behind one shop there were large ovens 'where nearly all the villagers used to have their bread baked on a certain day in the week'.

The wooden steps at Bispham leading from high cliffs to shore, in August 1915. Later they fell into disrepair. The primitive nature of this ancient hamlet was evident even then. For over a hundred years the village had one road running through from Hoo Hill to Cleveleys. A sea road from Norbreck had been swept away by tides long before.

A fire brigade drawn by horses was sent from Blackpool to deal with any fires in thatch or haystacks. Ancient Biscopham, as it is called in Domesday Book, covered 960 acres, an area greater than any settlement in the Hundred of Amounderness. Bispham-with-Norbreck existed long before Blackpool but later amalgamated with the famous seaside resort. The photograph dates from around the turn of the century.

The Miners' Home, Bispham, opened in 1927 by the Prince of Wales, had its foundation stone laid on 28 June 1925 by Colonel Pilkington of Haydock Colliery and Mr Thomas Greenall MP. The cost, £150,000, was raised by a levy of 1d. per ton on coal from the Lancashire and Cheshire coalfields.

The laundry at the Miners' Home is one of a series of photographs showing some of the then up-to-date amenities of this magnificent, purpose-built convalescent home. Facilities added later include three bungalows for paraplegic mineworkers. The home is now called the Lancashire and North Staffordshire Miners' Convalescent Home and the Lancashire Paraplegic Mineworkers' Holiday Unit.

Alderman Walker Taylor drives his wagonette and horses over Thornton level crossing by the Bay Horse Inn, *c.* 1918, when Mr Lawrenson was licensee. Holidaymakers were driven around the Fylde from Albert Road, Blackpool, where later Mr Taylor ran his first motor coaches, 'Pride of the Road'. These were cream and green, colours later adopted by Blackpool Corporation when it took over the service. Taylor's coaches were the first to run from Blackpool to Yorkshire.

Bispham parish church choir outing, 21 June 1939. The excursion was to Shrewsbury where a luncheon of kidney soup, whiting, roast sirloin, Yorkshire pudding, and fruit salad or apple Charlotte was served. Tea at 4 p.m. was brown or white bread and butter with cold tongue, jam and cakes. The excursion brochure contained a plan of interesting buildings in Shrewsbury.

London and North Western Railway Omnibus. This smart one-horse turn-out from 1905 met the trains coming to Thornton for Cleveleys station and quickly transported visitors to Cleveleys Hydro and other lodgings. In 1865 a station called Cleveleys was opened near the short-lived Ramper Road which had its name changed in 1905, and again in 1965 to Thornton Cleveleys.

Bispham Gala, 1928. Like those of other Fylde villages, this was a special annual summer occasion when most residents celebrated. These two ladies have decorated their babies' bassinets. Bicycles, horses and lorries were also decked out with paper flowers and ribbons. Neighbouring brass bands paraded and after the procession there were games and sports with prizes.

Bispham children's Sunday School outing to Lancaster, *c.* 1930. A Fylde longhouse can be seen in the background below the railway bridge advertising Loxham's of Lancaster. Canon Ward, a keen photographer, has set his camera and joined the group. Sitting in the centre is Mrs Ward, wearing a coat with fur collar.

Bispham church bible class outside the old vicarage in the early 1900s. On the next to back row the fourth lady from the right is Ellen Swarbrick. Canon Leighton sits behind the five in the front row. In those days the nearby Red Lion Inn had a bowling green and advertised 'Good Family Hot Pot'.

Bispham village, with a father taking his daughter to school, 1949. There was a free school in Bispham in 1621, a reference to 'Mr Bamber, Schoolmaster of Bispham', being made in that year. A thatched dwelling house, 14 acres of land and an allotment on Layton Hawes were granted to Mr Bamber, who improved his land greatly, making it worth £70 a year rental.

The Manchester Bank shown on the left in Bispham village was open on Thursdays at the time of this postcard (1927), when bicycles were growing in popularity. In 1892 the post and money order office was run by Mr Richard Cookson, letters arriving via Poulton-le-Fylde at 7.10 a.m. The posting house was at Joseph Foster's Albion Hotel.

The great snows of 1940 covered the country. The road through to All Hallows' church, Bispham, was dug out by American soldiers stationed in the district. The lady standing on the right is Mrs Ward, wife of Canon Ward. Snow drifted to the height of bedroom windows and livestock was buried.

Cliff Place, Bispham (1922), was a new development when the district was becoming popular for retirement. A series of photographs by Maurice P. Fitzgerald, commissioned by the Urban District Council, show the unmade state of roads such as Wharton Avenue, Thornton. Such was the rate of growth to meet demand for houses that road-making could not keep pace.

Two children outside the Thatched Café in Red Bank Road. The name originates from 'the red banks (marl cliffs) behind Rossall' where a ship from Barbados laden with sugar and cotton wool foundered in October 1702. The ship was eventually pounded to pieces by the waves but the cargo was taken to Squire Fleetwood's barn and Bispham chapel.

Bispham village. Beyond the thatched cottage with its cobble walls is a large Victorian house with barge boarding and advertisements. By now the school had been rebuilt under the scheme published by the Charity Commissioners in 1876. The church, which is thought to have existed in 1296, had been enlarged in 1881 to accommodate 320 people.

Norbreck tram station. A tramroad along the cliffs was developed by the Blackpool and Fleetwood Tramroad Co. Ltd, working alongside the Gynn Estate Co. Ltd, which was formed on 19 May 1897 by local businessmen to improve the coastal area. It was an immediate success.

Norbreck Hall Hydro. The old name for what all now refer to as The Norbreck is seen in this photograph showing the tram track. Norbreck Estate was planned by T.G. Lumb, opening up what had been called 'the wilds of Norbreck'. He also commissioned E.L. Lutyens to design the Cottage Exhibition, part of his 'City of the Fylde' notion.

Henry Thistleton outside No. 12, Alexander Grove, Thornton, in 1934. He was then 82. A long-standing resident of the Fylde, as were his family before him, he died two years later.

Abraham Barlow, a life-long Bispham resident, retired from his successful coal business at the age of 84. He gave £1,000 to found the Abraham Barlow Trust to provide lectures and concerts for the Bispham Community Association. This was a unique opportunity for all to enjoy the talents of such celebrities as the poet Vernon Scannell, and the oboist Evelyn Rothwell, the wife of Sir John Barbirolli.

The Cleveleys Hotel, *c.* 1900. The hotel can be seen behind the low-built, thatched cottages. A typical sea wall, constructed by using pebbles from the beach, divides the properties. It was to the Cleveleys Hotel that news of the sinking of the *Abana* in 1894 was brought.

Caravans in Bispham Road at the Urban District boundary looking west, with the bulk of Cleveleys Hydro in the background. When Cleveleys was rapidly being built up in the 1920s and 1930s, caravan dwellers, who had previously had the place to themselves, had to be moved.

Tay Pot Row. A group of cottages so named because of the inhabitants' reputation for brewing up from big black kettles kept constantly on the hob. Across the road, on the right, is the Gardeners Arms, a name corrupted from Gardner, a one-time innkeeper. A Thornton visitor sent this card in 1921.

Thornton parish church in the 1890s. The church pre-dates St Peter's at Fleetwood. Before 1840 babies from Fleetwood and district were brought here for christening. At one time private roads ran along two sides of the church and the parish stocks were close by. This photograph illustrates the changes that have taken place in church exterior and surroundings.

Thornton for Cleveleys railway station, formerly Ramper Road, in the 1920s. On the platform boys from Rossall School are wearing their summer uniform of Eton collars and straw hats.

A Thornton-le-Fylde country lane with a solitary man on a bicycle. This is not far away from Tay Pot Row where, like Ringley Sam, it was said of one cottager in rhyme: 'T'stead o' brewing his tay in a pot / He stewed it in a pan.' Early samples of tea sent to Fylde families were puzzling to them. One servant brewed tea with hot water and served up the leaves.

The New Promenade, Cleveleys. The works cost £30,000, and the promenade had its foundation stone laid by Councillor J. Rowbotham, chairman of the council, on 17 September 1927. A time capsule containing posters, town-planning map, official guide to Thornton-Cleveleys and copies of local newspapers was placed in a lead-lined oak casket which was then sealed. On the right can be seen the tents of a holiday camp for young men.

Victoria Road East. The Wignall Memorial Methodist church is on the left. One car and one bicycle point to the almost traffic-free days of the 1920s and 1930s. The church celebrated its fiftieth anniversary between 30 April and 8 May 1955. The Methodists had come a long way from the days when Missionary Holden wrote: 'I was sorely tried by the people of Thornton Marsh.'

The Square, Cleveleys, c. 1930. Victoria Road vanishes into the distance, and the photograph shows a good expanse of traffic-free road. But on the left is the sign 'garage', built on the site of thatched Woodbine Cottage, an indication of things to come in an area now carrying a heavy volume of traffic.

Queen Victoria Avenue, 1927. There was no highway to Thornton until Ramper Road, now called Victoria Road, was built of gravel over the marsh under an order called the Marsh Act Award, 1805. Thornton Marsh or Common Waste separated the sea from the river. Bold Fleetwood Hesketh was trying to keep the sea out of his land but floods still reached Parr's Lane, now Meadows Avenue.

Memorial Gardens, Thornton-le-Fylde. From here there was once an unbroken view to the windmill until the library and lecture hall were built. In the gardens is a war memorial for the eighty-four local men who died in the First World War.

Two girls enjoy a brisk sea at Cleveleys Breakwater. This Fred Anyon photograph from the late 1930s was one of those used in the Thornton-Cleveleys holiday guide. It is in the area of the bathing station and the moveable water slide.

Donkeys on the beach were once features of Cleveleys' foreshore but amusements have since moved into the town itself. From the little school on the Moss, with its boundary wall built of pebbles from the beach, Carleton scholars marched here for a treat on Royal Oak Day, 29 May. The photograph dates from around 1937.

The promenade and gardens, with Cleveleys Hydro in the distance, is yet another in the 1930s series of picture postcards. The Hydro has given way to a housing estate but was once a luxury hotel with tennis courts, resident orchestra, eighteen-hole golf course, swimming pool and remedial baths.

Jubilee Gardens, Thornton-Cleveleys, were opened by Lord Stanley in Coronation Year 1937, witnessed by dense crowds. A big procession, tea for pensioners at the Royal Hotel, free amusements for children and a visit from the Cotton Queen of Britain were all part of the celebrations Lord Stanley set in motion when he cut the ribbon on 1 May.

Jubilee Gardens on a brilliant summer day. Besides the paddling pool, the gardens also offered tennis courts, pitch and putt, and bowling. Lord Stanley himself bowled the first wood on the bowling green after the official opening and the Jubilee Gardens were an immediate success.

Jubilee Gardens pool, showing the attraction of water to children. Cleveleys beckoned as early as May 1785 when John Salthouse advertised in the *Manchester Mercury*, telling the world he had 'genteely fitted up the Inn or Bathing House called Cleeveleys'.

The Arena clock tower was one of the attractions introduced at the time of the Jubilee Gardens layout. In the nearby Arena concert parties performed daily throughout the season for what was advertised in the 1930s as 'the premier open-air theatre of the North'. Charlie and the Follies were popular. On Sundays came the Clifton Opera Singers.

Cleveleys beach in the 1930s, showing the large rowing boats that took visitors on sea trips. Pleasure boats for the public are no longer to be seen here. Sea angling, with the headquarters of a club closer to Bispham, is now more in demand.

Marsh Mill. A new oak beam, upon which the sails were to rest, was hoisted into position in July 1979. The six-storey mill, built by Bold Fleetwood Hesketh in 1794, measured 102 ft in circumference at its base and stood 110 ft high, with four wooden sails 35 ft long. On a cold day in October 1882, when John Barnes the miller was being buried, the sails began to turn in the wrong direction and had to be harnessed with heavy iron chains. The Barnes family, comprising eleven children, paid £75 half-yearly rental to Mr Tyler, who then owned the mill.

Atkinson's Meadow behind Marsh Mill features some fine horses being brought to the Mill Smithy. Other photographs show this field full of stooks of corn. In the mill yard was Jack Breckell's wheelwrights shop. At a public auction in October 1954 bidding for Marsh Mill and a detached house reached £2,250 but the lot was withdrawn from sale, as was another, the smithy and two cottages in the mill yard. Mr Goodall, auctioneer, remarked: 'The ghost is included in the lot,' but there were no takers. Marsh Mill was last used to grind corn in 1921.

Wardleys Ferry, Thornton. Passengers rang a bell or whistled for the ferryman. The ferry was in use when Squire Thomas Tyldesley travelled around the Fylde in the eighteenth century, for he mentions it in his diary. In the distance can be seen the warehouses, since demolished, which served Poulton when it was a port dealing in cheese, timber, guano and slaves. Mr Swarbrick was one of the ferrymen. His wife and daughter made Wardleys toffee, which was sought after by such visitors as these in 1920.

James Murray, photographed by Fylde photographer Fred Ash, came to work as a manager at Preesall Salt Works in 1889 when he was only 19. When the company was bought by ICI he stayed on, and later his descendants worked at Hill House, Thornton.

Mary Alice Collinge, photographed in 1901 at the age of 21, married James Murray seven years later. She had a brother, John Edmund, who emigrated to New Zealand.

Ranged under their church banner 'Praise to the Lord', a group from Wignall Memorial Methodist church on Victoria Road East, Thornton, photographed in the early 1900s after a performance of *The Village Wedding*. Seated in front are the Parkinson twins, Agnes and Grace, from the family of Poulton corn millers. Middle row, left to right: Mrs J. Breckell, Mrs Stafford, Mrs R. Wright, Miss Brierley, Miss Neild, Miss Smith, Mrs F. Pope, Mrs F. Thomas. Standing: Mrs Foxley, Miss Anne Higson, Mrs G. Wright, Miss Alice Harrison, Miss Clara Acornley, Mrs Norah Nelson, Miss Gertie Acornley, Mrs N. Cannan, Mrs W. Jolley, Mrs W. Brown, Mrs Bristow, Mrs J. Murray and Miss Edith Bristow.

Leaders and trustees of Wignall Memorial Methodist church, Victoria Road East, Thornton, in 1962. Left to right: J.W. Punshon, N. Robinson, G. Stott, J. McGrindle, T. Gillow, W.E. Tait, H.M. Hodson, A.E. Bevis, J.F. Tattersall, J.L. Rundle, J.E. Barker, A. Dalglish, W.J. Fyffe, T.F. Eaton, E.R. Gilfoy, F.G. Lewis, A.E. Barnes, N. Parr, B. Butler, W. Eastham, T.B. Eaton. The Revd H. Williams and the Revd W.R. Davies are also in the group.

Thornton First Methodist chapel. This chapel was built in 1789 on the desolate expanse of Thornton Marsh, a tract belonging to the Hesketh family. The first members were Rebecca Croft, Bradshaw Croft, Ben Wilding, John Bleasdale, Nanny Greenwood, and Richard and Betty Charnley. During the dark months worshippers arrived carrying horn lanterns. Gentleman farmer Bold Fleetwood Hesketh had a map of his Rossall demesne lands drawn up in 1799 by T. Varley, which included 'Thornton in the County of Lancaster'. He planned to enclose the marsh, drain it and produce better wheat crops as a result.

# Fleetwood

Ferry Dock, Fleetwood, early in this century, with bootblack boys.

The paddle steamer *Her Majesty* was used to head posters issued by the North Lancashire Steam Navigation Company on their timetables for the Fleetwood–Belfast run. It was printed by town pioneers Stanley Brothers, among the first to take premises on Dock Street. Frederick Kemp, who controlled the Navigation Company, himself used the iron steamship. It was making regular runs to Ireland in 1844 but was wrecked in 1849. The engraving also appeared with advertisements and booking details in the *Fleetwood Chronicle*.

Shipping scene, early 1870s. The sailing smacks silhouetted against the sky include: *Onward* FD 17, owned by R. Leadbetter; *Milo* FD 19, G. Miller; *White Rose* FD 21, R. Leadbetter; *Confidence* FD 48, W. Leadbetter; *Irish Lily* FD 50, J.H. Collins; *Ida* FD 51, R. Ashcroft; *Bluebell* FD 56, G. Miller.

Outbuildings, Rossall Hall Farm. When Fleetwood town was built the farm, situated at the gates of Rossall Hall and later known as Fleetwood Farm, supplied the manor house. Built of cobbles from the beach, it was demolished in the 1960s.

The Croft brothers, who were River Wyre ferrymen. John, William junior, John James and R. Rawlinson first used rowing boats and then bought thirteen sailing boats costing £30 each and a steam launch for forty-two passengers. The 1893 Fleetwood Improvement Act enabled the establishment of a regular service.

Mr R. Forrester Addie, cricket bat over shoulder, was a supporter of Fleetwood Cricket Club and associated with the town as lawyer from the late nineteenth century. He then left to become Recorder at the County Court in Salford. He played as fast bowler until 1904 and returned in retirement as president of the club, 1936–41.

*Richard Warbrick*, a topsail schooner built at Fleetwood, was painted by J. Semple of Belfast in 1864. A contemporary description at the launching of the *John Gibson* shows that of twenty-five Fleetwood-built vessels all were still in good condition except the *Manchester*, which was lost with all hands in 1867. 'Decorated with a new set of flags, the *John Gibson* was a pretty sight. At one o'clock work began on knocking the supports from under her. The daggers were knocked away 25 minutes later, under the personal supervision of John Gibson. Immediately she commenced to glide down the ways and was christened by Miss Porter, daughter of Edmund Porter, shipowner.' Fitted out with sails and stores, official number 73756, classed A 1 at Lloyds, she lay near the China Clay warehouse and, like the *Emily* and *Richard Warbrick* carried china clay from Fowey. The *John Gibson* was lost off Dover on 11 January 1926.

*Harriet* FD 111, the most famous of all Fleetwood fishing smacks, held the record for a catch of sole and survived the fiercest storms. She was built in 1893 at a cost of £1,200 for Richard Leadbetter who owned a large fish shop and the Bell Restaurant.

Early fishing boat enters the Wyre as the cabin boy trims the lamp. Another of his duties was to cut shag tobacco and prepare clay pipes for the crew. Primitive conditions in the 1870s made the job hazardous.

West Street Congregational church. Before it was built twelve members gathered at Mrs Garner's Flag Street cottage. Thomas Drummond commenced building in July 1847 'a neat brick structure with side buttresses and a castellated tower', which was opened on 31 May 1848. A century later Marks & Spencer occupied the site.

Queen's Terrace, designed by classical architect Decimus Burton, was finished by 1845. ('For bell-hanging – Queen's Terrace in 1841, Mr Woodward – charge £29 10s 0d.') Renamed Bleasdale Court and Wyre View, after lying empty in the 1960s these elegant town houses were converted into flats – but the terrace retains its importance as a listed building.

Buoy in the River Wyre. Captain Henry Mangles Denham was entrusted with charting the approach to Fleetwood port. Eight black buoys and five red buoys with one cage buoy were involved in early charting. In 1840 Denham issued his *Remarks and Sailing Directions for Approaching and Navigating the Sea Reaches of Wyre and Estuary,* which was much praised by the Tidal Commissioners.

*Wyre Majestic,* ship's bell. One of a class of four built for Wyre Trawlers at Cockerham's of Selby, *Wyre Majestic* was completed in 1956. These trawlers had distinctive names and separate squat funnels. *Wyre Majestic* was lost off Jura in Islay Sound, striking the rocks at high speed. This made it impossible to move her, even with the help of a Glasgow tug.

SS *Duke of Clarence* sailed on the Fleetwood–Londonderry service, a short-lived arrangement compared with Fleetwood–Belfast, which ran for eighty-five years. The Londonderry service, resumed in 1903 for carrying cattle, was finally terminated in 1912 as demand declined.

*Falcon*, pilot schooner (1894–1972), was built by Nicholson and Marsh at Glasson Dock. In 1932 James Fleck reported: 'She was a lovely, well-kept schooner, her decks varnished twice a year.' Built originally for Robert Gerrard, this clipper-bowed vessel was dashed to pieces in a gale off Cornwall.

# AN APPEAL!

## EFFECTS OF THE STORM, OCTOBER 2nd, 189

### SOME OF THE DROWNED FISHERMEN, AND A GROUP OF FATHERLESS CHILDREN.

In the Storm of October 2nd, 1895, there were Five Fleetwood Fishing Boats Wrecked, involving the loss of 11 men, 8 of whom we married. 8 WIDOWS and 37 CHILDREN (32 being under 14 years of age) are left unprovided for.

Subscriptions on behalf of the Widows and Children should be sent to any of the following:—

Councillor DAVIES, J.P., Chairman
Councillor R. C. WARD, Hon. Treasurer    Relief Committee,
Mr. R. F. ADDIE, Hon. Secretary    Fleetwood

Appeal poster, following the great storm of 2 October 1895. The December 1894 storm had wrecked the *Abana*, *Skulda* and *Furo*, and involved the fishing smacks *Red Rose*, *Mayflower*, *Surprise* and *Petrel*. The *Falmouth* grounded at Rossall Point, the bodies of the crew, including the captain's wife and child, being washed up later. The lifeboat had its main mast, 10 in thick, snapped like a clay pipe. 'We might as well have pulled at the Tower as tried to use oars,' said Mr Rimmer who rigged up a spar as main mast and set sails to reach Fleetwood. In the same great gale the Fylde Rubber Works in London Street was blown down and the grain elevator cracked.

Crew of the *Duke of York*, number 104233, in the days when Fleetwood–Belfast steamers were 'fitted up in much the same style as the famous American liners'. All personnel were determined to make the service second to none. Following the pioneer steamer *Duke of Connaught*, the *Duke of York* came into service in 1894. As the magnificent screw steamers were introduced, the paddle steamers departed. Names of some of the crew are, seated: Mr Piper, Mr Cowell, A. Carden (pantry boy), Mrs McCaffery, and Mr Wilks. Hornby Leadbetter (cook) stands at the back. In 1911 the *Duke of York* was withdrawn and sold to Turkey.

Fleetwood's Lower Light and masted barque is typical of the shipping scene ten years after the opening of Wyre Dock when cargo trade was at its height. Ships came and went on every tide. When the dock was full, this was indicated by a special flag. Details of each vessel were entered in heavy, leather-bound ledgers.

East Street. The Index Book records that on 2 September 1899 Mr H.H. Nickson was commissioned to prepare 500 photo engravings. This photograph includes Hodgson's stores, the Congregational church, and Walmsley's, one of the oldest businesses, opposite which is the Co-operative Society's emporium.

Fleetwood Promenade, photographed by Mr H.H. Nickson. 'Methley', the end house on the right, dates from 1845 when Mount Terrace was built. The Mount, originally the highest of a chain of sandhills, most of which were washed away by the sea, was anciently known as Tup or Starr Hill.

Mr Oldham, station master, with his black spaniel, which accompanied him everywhere, is photographed on the Docks in the early 1900s. In his top hat and frock coat, sporting a rose in his buttonhole, he patrolled the fine railway station and saw off the Isle of Man boats.

Parade of the Border Brigade, Fleetwood Camp. 'Fleetwood awoke one morning to find itself famous as the seat of the School of Musketry,' wrote the Revd Charles Hesketh in 1864. The government had bought the North Euston Hotel for this purpose in 1859. Soldiers, encampments and a rifle range became part of the scene.

Pleasure boat stage and esplanade. This photograph features the lifeboat house, the Decimus Burton-designed Lower Light, North Euston Hotel and Customs Watch House. Along the front is a row of ornamental cannon placed there by Sir Peter Hesketh Fleetwood to grace the new town. The typical pleasure boat, which probably sailed to Wardleys, was the type owned by Hornby Cowell, boatman. The *Teetotaller* No. 2 was 'licensed to ply for hire within the limits of the Act'. Hornby was also gamekeeper to Sir Peter Hesketh Fleetwood. When the baronet drove to the station from Rossall Hall he sent word ahead that farm gates must be opened in readiness for the crested carriage.

Fishing fleet in Wyre Dock. Steam trawling made phenomenal progress at Fleetwood because of its commodious harbour and geographical position in relation to the fishing grounds. Coal and dock dues were low, catches excellent. East-coast owners also sent trawlers to the 'Fishing Port of the West'. *Thrush* GY 114, from Grimsby, is having its fish landed by 'lumpers'. In 1914 over 60,000 tons of fish were landed in 3,917 trips, a sevenfold increase on 1904.

Fishing at Fleetwood evokes many memories. Charles Martland, for example, remembers the following: 'We children loved our Dad and we were proud that he was a skipper. We would stand on the ferry slip and watch the ship pass up river and he would give us a blow on the steam whistle to show that he had seen us waving. . . . Carrying his oil-skin shirt bag with the fancy Turk's head knots and intricate plaits, he would come home bringing sea gear that needed to be washed.

'I was fascinated by the tattoos on his arms. One was a buxom Edwardian lady draped in a Union Jack who, when he flexed his muscles, performed the hula. He would never sail on a Friday or harm a seagull and the word pig had never to be uttered. He belted one unfortunate right round the ship for the crime of red-leading a seagull. Way back from windjammer days, he told me of a shark's tail being hung from the bowsprit to ensure fair winds.'

Co-operative Wholesale Society boot and shoe shop in Kent Street, *c.* 1912. Outside are the staff. Left to right: Miss Whittaker, Bill Worden, Jack Parkinson, 'Doc' Cookson and Ambrose Holdsworth. The men, in their long aprons, did repairs and clogging.

Billingsgate House, Leadbetter's fish shop, in North Albert Street, 1927. To this shop came Judge Parry, who wrote delightful children's stories about Fleetwood such as *Butterscotia*. Other well-known shops were Cartmell's where boy scouts bought their uniform, Barnfield's cake shop and Crow's drapers, where Lilla Richardson was paid 6d. a week as apprentice milliner.

Fleetwood railway station, planned by the London and North Western Railway Company's architect C.W. Green, opened on 15 July 1883. It became celebrated for its floral displays and such facilities as its first-class refreshment room, dining room and connecting walkway to the quay.

Fishing fleet leaving Fleetwood. This postcard sent in 1912 shows fishing smacks with their freshly barked sails making for Morecambe Bay. Some sold their catches from the beach; others raced for port. The Fleetwood Fishing Vessel Owners' Association was formed in 1907. The process of barking stiffened sails and dyed them red.

Music teacher on the promenade, 1903. J. Grindrod, teacher of pianoforte, organ and singing, may have known the gentleman in the centre, also a music teacher, promenading with his wife. The recently completed esplanade is empty apart from a baby's bassinet.

Tramcar near Pharos Lighthouse. The Blackpool and Fleetwood Tramroad Acts 1896 and 1898 led to a system that still draws enthusiasts from as far away as San Francisco. Miss F. Fish, on the right, aunt of the late alderman and mayor, Mrs Rowntree, stands with her friend by Car 14 in 1910.

Empty promenade with Master Nickson. This wide promenade replaced the carriage drive and promenade along the shore from the North Euston Hotel to Mount Terrace which was pounded by seas and fell into dilapidation. The opening of the promenade and Fielden Library was celebrated by a Grand Fête on 10 September 1887.

*ST Eddystone* FD 372 passes ferry boat *Onward* in the 1930s. There are many stories attached to trawlers. For example, the 438-ton trawler *Kirkella*, launched in 1936, later became the *Moorsom*. Bought by Cevic Fishing Company, she was renamed *St Benedict* in 1955 but changed again to *Reneva*, a name based on R. Neave, a director of the firm.

Coal wagon at the foot of Pharos Lighthouse. Tons of coal arrived in the 1920s; this lorry load was destined for houses. On the dock was a 680-ft coaling wharf built by Lancashire and Yorkshire Railway equipped with a 2 ½-ton electric transporter designed by George Hughes, the company's chief mechanical engineer.

Steam trawlers in dock, 1912. The coal miners' strike left eighty trawlers lying idle. The foundation of the modern industry was laid in 1891 when *Lark* arrived in the charge of Harry Bird. Councillor Wallace Carter Frith persuaded Moody and Kelly of Grimsby to experiment, which led to the timber pond being made into the fish dock.

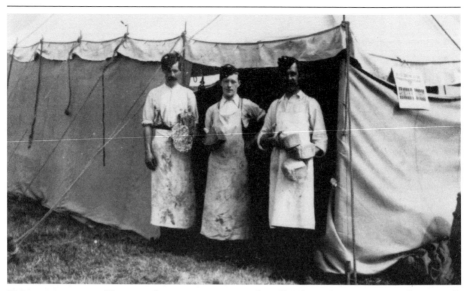

Volunteer camp at Fleetwood, grocery stores and staff. The Atkinson series of postcards was issued for volunteer soldiers to send home in the early years of the century. Hundreds of tents were pitched in the fields of Rossall Grange Farm, the portering of ammunition to the Hutments Barracks being done by John W. Wilson and Sons of Kent Street.

The Fish Dock, 1912. One of a series of photographs commissioned by Dock Manager Tom Blacklidge, it shows the debris that had collected in the dock. Periodically, dredging operations brought up winches, nets and otter doors which crews had thrown overboard under extreme conditions because of their fear of putting to sea.

Wyre Dock from roof of dock office, 1953. MV *Ferriday* often docked in Fleetwood with cargoes of calcium carbide destined for the ICI factory at Burn Naze. In the foreground, tied up, is the steam trawler *Frobisher*.

Promenade, North Euston Hotel and Pier. In 1920 when this photograph was taken, beyond the hotel to the left was the football ground and a line of hoardings. On 11 October 1899 Fleetwood Urban District Council agreed to the loss of part of the fore-shore so that a pier could be erected.

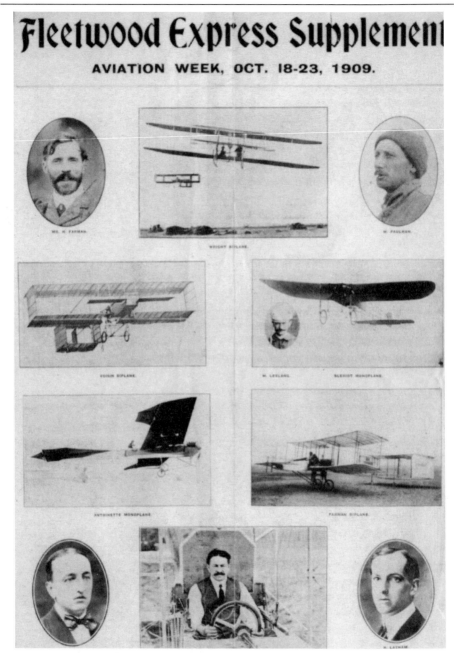

# Fleetwood Express Supplement

## AVIATION WEEK, OCT. 18-23, 1909.

Fleetwood Express Supplement – Aviation Week. The event, held from 18 to 23 October 1909, was only the second such in Britain. It was advertised widely in the Fylde and thousands turned up even though the weather was atrocious. The French contestants took the prize money.

First ELRFA Battalion landing at Fleetwood, 1 August 1908. This is another in the series issued by the YMCA and shows the fine station that replaced the 1840 original opposite the Crown Hotel. Thousands of soldiers and civilians passed through its concourse. It was demolished in February and March 1969.

Strike scenes – hundreds stranded, 1926. The coal miners' strike and General Strike led to travellers from the Isle of Man being stranded at Fleetwood. Cinemas were opened all night for mothers and children to take refuge.

The Sunshine Home, Rossall, or Cinderella Home, photographed in the 1940s, was inspired by Gracie Fields, who wanted poor children to have seaside holidays. It is now Rossall Hospital for Geriatrics.

Victoria Pier was completed in 1910 after many attempts. Mr Tickell of Fleetwood issued this commemorative postcard. The event was teamed with the exhibition of the Convict Ship, raised from Sydney Harbour, at Jubilee Pier.

An accident at the Ice Factory Extension, 1913. Before the factory was built supplies of ice had been brought in by ship, which was very expensive. Regular callers were SS *Sjoguttan*, the first to enter Wyre Dock on behalf of Moody and Kelly, *Krosfond* from Norway, *Regina* and *Laboremus*.

Box-making at Wyre Dock, 1912. Thousands of boxes were needed for the fish trade. A conveyor ran from the fish stages, horses and carts stood by railway lines, and fish was then despatched to London's Billingsgate market in less than twenty-four hours via the London and North Western Railway.

Mr Cowell on board *Lady Moyra*. The 'Barrow Boats' were very popular. Many visitors were taken from there to Lake Windermere or Coniston; others toured Furness Abbey ruins. The Furness Railway Manager, Harry Aslett, offered cheap combined train and boat fares.

On board *Lady Evelyn*. A visitor with the pastor from Mount Road Methodist church (right) is *en route* to Barrow for the Lake District on 23 September 1909. Photographs taken on the outward trip could be collected on the return.

SS *Lady of Mann* leaves Fleetwood. In May 1992 the 150th anniversary of the start of a weekly service from Fleetwood to the Isle of Man for passengers and goods was celebrated. *Mona's Isle*, a paddle steamer commanded by Edward Quayle, made the first trip.

*Having a " High Old Time " at Fleetwood*

The 1909 Aviation Week led to a spate of postcards in 1910, such as 'flying' visitors over Wyre Dock. Cantilever cranes which handled 50 tons of coal an hour, masted barques and steamers are part of the scene below.

Coronation festivities, 1911. Mr Rawcliffe's coal wagon was one of many floats that celebrated the Coronation. Peace celebrations after the First World War were even more elaborate, the high spot being a bonfire on the beach opposite the Mount. At that time the tram standards in the middle of Lord Street were being altered. The wooden blocks removed from the paving were collected in trolleys by boys who bore off as many as they could carry for a halfpenny a trip. The Council provided fireworks and at midnight George Cowell, slipway manager, lined up children in readiness with red and green flares to spell out 'Peace'.

Fleetwood and Knott End Ferry. The photograph shows *Wyresdale* and across the estuary can be seen Knott End Railway, where passengers could board trains for Garstang. 'Steamers running every few minutes' was the slogan in the 1920s when the adult fare each way was 2d. In 1927 almost 800,000 passengers and over 11,000 bicycles were carried. Occasionally on board was a travelling showman with his dancing bear who toured Fylde villages. There was an amusing scale of charges for many types of merchandise, including pigs, goats, coffins and wooden dressers. *Wyresdale*, the largest steamer, had twin screws and a crew of three and could carry 250 passengers.

Trawlers with grain elevator in background. *Teroma* is berthed alongside FD 300.
Trawlers were bunkered at a special berth 550 ft long, opposite but well away from the
fish market. The finest bunker coal was delivered by wagons at the ship's side.

Custom House and Brick Terrace, 1964. Photographed from the railway colonnades
where crowds queued for the Isle of Man boat, the Decimus Burton-designed Custom
House of 1840 can be seen in the centre of Lower Queen's Terrace (Brick Terrace).

The Packing Shed, in the 1920s. Gutted fish are being taken from Molly hampers and packed with ice in fish boxes. Ninety smacks operated until steam trawlers reduced their numbers. Fishing firms included Devon Steam Fishing Company, Taylor and Tomlinson, Sun Steam Fishing Company and Clifton Steam Fishing Company. Related firms were Gourock Rope Company, Cosalt and Trawler Supply Company. Mr Harry Melling, a trawler owner, was the first to auction fish himself. The daily sale of catches by auction commenced in 1906. Aluminium kits holding 10 stones of fish replaced the hampers.

Launch of the ferry boat *Wyresdale*. The vessel was built by Robertsons Ltd, and the launch was a great occasion in Fleetwood. It was a day for best hats, coats and walking canes. In the background is the dock slipway. Front, far left and next to the bearded gentleman, is Theodore Clegg from Ye Olde Bacca Shoppe, once a Mayor of Fleetwood. Another well-known tradesman, Mr Priestley, draper, stands under the letter T of Robertsons. Immediately behind the bollard is Charles Saer, headmaster, who also became an alderman and mayor of the town. Harry Chapman is the little boy.

The great storm and flood at Fleetwood occurred late at night on 29 October 1927, and engulfed most of the town. This photograph from a specially commissioned set shows some of the hundreds of logs that were swept down Lord Street from Keay's Sawmills. Clearing up was a monumental task. Six people died, along with sheep, dogs and cattle. Homes were flooded to ceiling height. A Flood Disaster Fund was raised to assist families who had lost furniture, clothes, carpets, and other effects. Cities and towns from all over the country helped by sending supplies, for example 'The Leeds Convoy'. Hovis delivered bread, Calverts carbolic and disinfectant, and coal came from Lancashire collieries.

The Queen's Theatre or 'Old Gaff' in Adelaide Street was demolished in the 1960s. It was very popular in its day, George Formby senior being one of many performers. Mr Crookall, a farmer, had two seats made into one to accommodate his bulk.

Adelina Patti poster. The coming of La Diva, Madame Patti, for her first and only appearance in the Fylde was hailed as the greatest concert of the century. She enthralled audiences with her encore, 'Home Sweet Home'.

Sea defences were breached on 4 December 1954. Fleetwood's Silver Jubilee mayor in 1958, Councillor H.A. Baker, referred to 'the tremendous programme of sea defence works'. High tides caused the damage shown. Walking together are surveyor Mr Melville and Mr Tom Gerrard.

Mending nets on Jubilee Pier. Mr R. Wright, originally from Marshside, is net-braiding. Generations of Wrights have been fishermen and lifeboatmen, the family having come to Fleetwood when receding tides at Southport threatened its livelihood.

Fleetwood Cricket Club team, 1921. Cricket was played on the Warren in the 1840s and the club formed in 1891 featured well-known local names: clergymen, schoolmasters, tradesmen, railway officials and men from the shipping companies such as R.C. Ward, L.G. Humphries, P. Forrest, J. Gaulter, W.H. Ashton, J.H. Kean and J. Lofthouse. This 1921 team played at Warrenhurst Park. Left to right: Umpire Jack Wright, Joseph Ashworth, F. Mitchell, A. Ramsdale, W.P. Lilwall, T.S. Leach, F. Threlfall, N. Humphries, J. Calderbank, Ernest Wilks, Clive Addie, Bill Dickinson, and H. Dickinson.

Visit of King George VI and Queen Elizabeth, 1938. Behind the King and Queen in Fleetwood's Marine Hall are Mayor and Mayoress Charles and Mrs Saer with the Town Clerk. A cosy touch is provided by the postman delivering telegrams. There was a great gathering of schoolchildren, who sang for the royal visitors. The visit was also an opportunity to look at the recently completed foreshore amenities provided by the Borough, which had achieved this status in Charter Year 1933.

Approaching the lock gates, 1973. From the formation of the Fleetwood Fishing Company in 1841 grew the great fishing industry which made Fleetwood the largest fishing port on the north-west coast and the third most important in England. One of the best known advertisements issued by the Fleetwood Fishing Vessel Association reads: 'Fleetwood fish is the finest, freshest and firmest, free from disease, found full fifty fathoms deep in the flowing, foaming ocean by famous fishermen. Forms an ideal food, feeds the brain and fulfils all functions of food. Faddists are funny fellows but only the foolish fail to fry and feast on Fleetwood fish.'

Charlie Martland, angling in the estuary, moves down Wyre in an old naval whale boat in the 1960s. These good craft, 28 ft long, 6 ft in beam, sailed fast with five oarsmen. Mr Martland was the first full-time boatman at Fleetwood Nautical College. The tin trunk contains fishing gear.

*Robert Hewett* and *Wyre Revenge* are tied up in Wyre Dock in 1973 because of the slump in the fishing industry following the Cod Wars with Iceland. The 391-ton *Boston Lightning* was sold to an East Coast firm, which also bought *Boston Crusader* and *Ssafa*.

The Ice House on Wyre Dock, finished *c.* 1908, served the industry for many years but modern stern trawlers like the *Junella* (J. Marr and Son Ltd), one of the two biggest in Britain, were to freeze all or part of the catch at sea and land it in fresh-frozen condition.

Roasting an ox for the mayor, 1969. The feast is for the mayor-elect Jonathan Neild, known to some as 'Mr Fleetwood'. Old inhabitants recall an ox-roasting on land near Warren Farm in 1920 done by two local butchers, Messrs Bennett and Williams.

The model yacht lake, one of the foreshore amenities built in the 1930s, was the largest in Europe. Today enthusiasts come from all over the world to compete in the summer.

Mr C. Hargreave, grocer and dairyman, is seen outside his shop with his polished milk float and horse decked with rosettes, ready to join a Hospital Saturday Procession. Nobby Clarke on his hobby horse was another familiar participant in the 1920s.

Fire at J. Marr and Son Ltd, 4 May 1919. Wyre Dock had its own fire brigade but on this occasion the town force was also needed. Gradige's timber fire raised a two-day pall of smoke, but the worst fire of all was when the pier burned down.

Club and canteen for HM Forces. The Church Army operated in Fleetwood's Adelaide Street in 1941. This drive was backed by Winston Churchill who urged greater and greater war effort to speed up victory. 'I am sure your appeal will be generously assisted. The Church Army is an institution.' His letter is on display.

Winches and warps on stern trawler, in 1969. This shows the amount of gear needed for a deep-sea fishing expedition. Fleetwood trawlers played a brave part in the two World Wars. *Hayburn Wyke* was torpedoed in the English Channel; *Donna Nook* sank after collision engaging an E-boat; *Barbara Robertson* was sunk by a U-boat, and the *Gava* assisted in the evacuation from Dunkirk. One of the first of the ships in Stanley Harbour in the Falklands War was the freezer *Junella*, the newest of the fleet.

Inshore fishing boat and ferry boat. *Bourne May* awaits inshore fishing boat N 65 before setting off from Ferry Dock in the 1960s. The Bourne Arms Hotel, known for its tender steaks and home-made ice cream, awaited the passengers.

*Stella Marina.* The Isle of Man boats still sail from the pier shown in this picture. The *Stella Marina* was a white Norwegian vessel that made trips to the Isle of Man for a short time in the 1960s. However, her shallow draught made for uncomfortable crossings when the Irish Sea was rough.

The last mayor-making at Fleetwood was an historic occasion at the Marine Hall before local government boundary changes and the creation of the Borough of Wyre in 1974. Featured are D.B. Timms, Borough Librarian, C. Rothwell, Deputy Borough Librarian, the Revd Trevor Southgate, vicar of St Peter's church, and the late Mrs Southgate. Floral displays by Mr Chantler of the Parks Department filled the stage. Robes, mayoral chains of office and the bearing of the heavy, enamelled civic mace were noteworthy features of this now-defunct annual occasion that had been held in Fleetwood since 1933.

Lancashire and Yorkshire Railway 'Dreadnought' locomotive. An Enthusiasts' Special to Blackpool on 1 July 1951, a few days before this locomotive was scrapped. Fleetwood station often saw these powerful four-cylinder 4–6–0s, derived from George Hughes' design and built at Horwich in 1908.

The last passenger train from Fleetwood, 1970. Among the passengers are Mr Langhorne and a group of Fleetwood Grammar School boys. Wyre Dock appeared as a new station in Bradshaw's timetable in January 1886 but full use was not made of it until 1900. When the main station closed on 16 April 1966, Wyre Dock station took over.

St Peter's parish church group, assembled to discuss diocesan matters. Standing, left to right: W. Waddington, Joe Sutton, H. Chapman, Mr Swarbrick, Mr Jellenden, Mr T. Longworth and H. Dandy. Seated: Miss Stanley, Mrs Watson, Mrs Bennett, Mrs H. Forshaw, Mr Womersley, the Revd Mr Stanton (the vicar), W. Hancock, Miss Roskell, Miss Cowell, Mrs Stanton and Mr Blacklidge. Decimus Burton chose the traditional site on raised ground in the centre of town for St Peter's, the building of which began in 1840. The Fleetwood-on-Wyre Certificate Book gives details of costs: enclosure wall £341; gas fittings £23 11s. 4d.; bell £34; chapel £2,700 (it was originally termed a chapel of ease); tower and spire £637.

# Across the River

View from top of Pharos Lighthouse, 1952.

Pier and ferry, Knott End, on a 1917 Sankey postcard after a choppy crossing. The ferry to Knott End ran from the old stone jetty opposite Whitworth Institute and was reached by the iron footbridge from Adelaide Street until the ferry dock was made. The landing stage at Knott End was erected in 1897, the first manager being Thomas Newton Crook. After 1893 *Playfair* and *Guarantee* were taken over by Fleetwood UDC and were later superseded by larger, well-type boats with central upright boilers and single-screw engines. The ferry steamer *Onward*, which cost £938, followed *Lune*; then came *Progress* and *Bourne May*, which in 1930 was still in commission with the *Pilling* and the *Wyresdale*.

St Bernard's-on-Sea. An attempt to change the name of Knott End to enhance its attractiveness as a seaside resort was not successful. This 1899 photograph shows Dolly's Cottage on the right, where Dolly served teas to visitors who were kept amused by the colourful language of her parrot.

Wyre View, Knott End was built by Dolly's son, Thomas Riley, a successful contractor in North Fylde. This 1916 postcard shows the garage from which the first Knott End Motors ran to meet ferry boats for tours of Over-Wyre.

Hackensall Hall, known by country people as Hackensha, derived from Haakon's Hough, is embowered in trees. The Great and Little Knotts, heaps of rocks which were removed when Captain Denham ordered improvements to be made for navigation of the River Wyre, were Scandinavian in origin. It is thought that the Norse invader Haakon landed here to set up his first homestead. A descendant, Geoffrey de Hackinsall, had the right of wreck of the sea allowed to him by King John when three casks of wine were washed up at Knott End. Geoffrey allowed a fishery in the River Wyre to support the canons of Cockersand Abbey. The Hall is of seventeenth-century origin and has a stone dated 1685 bearing the initials of Richard and Anne Fleetwood, who used the house when Rossall Hall was flooded.

Roger Collinson, travelling tailor, on his North Fylde rounds, is near Churchtown, in Cock Robin Lane. Calling at farms and isolated houses, he would measure for suits and long skirts, making them up from his customers' own materials for less than £2. This was taken in 1908 when Danby Eteson was proprietor of the Horns Inn.

The ferry, Knott End, in the early years of this century, showing many kinds of craft and boys with buckets and spades. Across the river can be seen the North Euston Hotel, the lighthouse and the lifeboat house.

W. Roskell, photographed in 1909, was born on 22 May 1833 at Quail Holme, Knott End. This was the home of his maternal great, great grandfather, Richard Silcock, a prominent North Fylde landowner. Quail Holme was one of the large houses pointed out to tourists.

Mr and Mrs Evan Jemson got around North Fylde on this motorbike and sidecar. Mr Jemson was for a time surveyor for the Garstang Rural District Council. The photograph dates from the early 1900s and shows the fashions of the day.

Dolly's Cottage, Knott End, *c.* 1910. A local washerwoman is at work. Sheets, shirts, underskirts, pillows and bolster cases were whitened on the thick hedges of back gardens close to the sea.

A motor charabanc advertises 'Grand Country Drive, Pilling Old Village and District, fare 1 shilling return'. It is drawn up ready for boarding by trippers who would later enjoy teas at the Saracen's Head, Mrs Simpson's Refreshment Rooms or Irving Jackson's New Golden Ball.

Camp of the First Cheshire Volunteers, Knott End. North Fylde country, with its acres of fields and farmland, made good camping areas for detachments of soldiers during the summer months. This photograph dates from between the World Wars.

Saddler's shop, Knott End, with Dick Shepherd, in 1912. Dick was the village saddler from 1886 to 1923 and in this small, self-supporting rural community played an important part, supplying spades, brushes, horse collars, baskets and rope.

The directors of the Knott End Railway are having a celebratory dinner on 8 July 1923. Its shareholders, however, did not fare very well when the LMS successfully negotiated to take over their company. For every £100 of Knott End ordinary stock they received only 125s. of LMS ordinary stock. Passenger services were withdrawn on 31 March 1930.

Arrival of the Fourth West Riding RFA at Knott End station in 1908. Travelling via Garstang, these troops had target practice firing at the many wrecks lying on Pilling sands. Old residents recall collecting spent cartridges.

Knott End from the east. This 1899 photograph shows how the small community became increasingly popular when it became 'a rising health resort'. Firm sands, bracing breezes and the glorious sunsets sung about by Fylde poet Gisborne added more interest and the advent of the railway made for easier communication. Boarding houses were built and shops such as Preston's Central Supply Stores catered for 'Picnic and Choir Parties'. H. Hawksworth of the Knott End Tobacco Stores had a large assortment of cigarette brands, meerschaum, briar, cherrywood and clay pipes, and 'walking sticks and soldiers' canes in great variety'.

Road leading from the Ferry Works at Knott End. The photograph was taken on 21 June 1901 by H.H. Nickson. The *Fylde Advertiser* printed Mr E. Rogers' advertisement: 'Parties staying at Fleetwood or visitors for the day will find it an agreeable change to cross the Ferry and visit the hotel.' The Bourne Arms was well known for its home-made ice cream, 'wines, spirits and malt liquors of the best qualities, parties supplied with tea, coffee and other refreshments. Plain teas ninepence each and Bowling Green attached kept in excellent condition.' Many times shipwrecked mariners struggled exhausted to the Bourne Arms, an inn situated on the edge of Pilling Sands.

Ben Butler, Knott End carrier, stands outside the Working Men's Club, *c.* 1912. In the background is Dolly's Cottage. Ben walked to Blackpool every day to deliver his goods.

W. Hamnett, North Fylde farmer, sends 2,000 chicks to Roumania from Blackpool Airport in 1931, a pioneer experiment in poultry rearing. 'A constant supply of Spring chickens' was offered by James Parkinson of The Mount, Preesall.

Pilling Village Brass Band outside Mrs Taylor's, a grocer and tobacconist, Highfield House, in 1908. She also sold toys and picture postcards. The occasion may be an Empire Day or the Coffee Feast.

A funeral cortège, Preesall, includes a glass-sided hearse with two coachmen. Cut flowers, crosses and wreaths could be supplied by James Parkinson, whose premises were on the main road between Knott End and Preesall: 'Visitors can spend a pleasant time in the beautiful gardens.'

Stalmine Hall, home of Cornelius Bourne in the 1840s, has now been turned into flats and an ancient yew tree has been destroyed. An 1830 letter from the Hall to William and Matthew Lewtas, timber merchants, refers to logs being floated down the River Wyre: 'I have to address you on the conduct of your three men who were yesterday conducting a craft of two. I sent word to be careful as possibly could when rafting timber past my weirs. The men aboard the raft yesterday from downright carelessness ran foul of the weir.' This sort of behaviour could damage the salmon ladders situated at various points in the days when the river had a plentiful supply of salmon. Stalmine was known as 'the flower garden of the Fylde' in the nineteenth century.

Old cottages, Preesall, in the early 1900s. The lords of the manor at Preesall were the Ellestons of Parrox Hall. These old cottages would originally have constituted a typical Fylde longhouse. The family occupied one end, livestock the other. Clay, wattle and daub, sea pebbles and thatch went into the construction. Strength was added by the clay and straw being trampled by horses before building. The village school at Preesall, built in 1695, was endowed by the Hesketh family.

The Saracen's Head, Preesall, in the early 1900s. The public house was run by Mr Child, who supplied luncheons to wagonette parties. A wine lodge next door catered for others. In front of the Saracen's Head the dancing bear performed in its tour of North Fylde.

Salt mine workers, Preesall, worked at the brine pumping stations in connection with the Preesall salt mines, an industry carried on by the United Alkali Company. In later years this activity led to alarming subsidence.

Thatched cottages at Damside, Taylors Lane, with the carrier's cart outside in 1903, were what town and city visitors came to see. The wheelwrights shop is on the left close to the blacksmiths as these two craftsmen worked together.

The pond by Pilling Hall, with an old farm gate and haystack in the background. This was a playground for schoolchildren in the 1900s; in 1969 it was visited fleetingly by a solitary pink flamingo.

A North Fylde farming scene, *c.* 1919. This is now recaptured at the Fylde Country Museum, Woods Lane, Pilling, on Mr Lawrenson's Southwoods Hill Farm. A working Marsden reaper and binder produces a traditional load such as this stacked on the haycart.

Traditional Fylde pig table. Four men and a boy attend a pig-killing at Pilling, *c.* 1909. Encouraged by William Cobbett in the eighteenth century, almost every household in the Fylde reared a pig.

Jack Hornby and Richard Jenkinson are working with their 'torf' barrow, which was specially made for the job. By August or September the turf was dry enough to build into a howk or round robin. Small turf mounds were known as memos. Two men working together, one delving and one 'putting out', could produce a 'fall' of 560 turves in one hour.

Peat Stack at Easham House Farm, *c.* 1960, with John Bradshaw carting turves in his strong barrow. For centuries Pilling Moss, 'boundless as God's grace', supplied tenant farmers for their own use. Saleable peat was dug by professional 'torf delvers'.

'Mrs Bleasdale's'. Zillah, draper and grocer ('ice cream made on the premises'), stands at the door of her Pilling shop, *c.* 1906. This industrious lady also served teas to visitors keen to see 'a genuine Fylde peasant'.

Moss Cottages, Pilling, 1904. From left to right: William Hornby, William Douglas Isles, Miss Betty Isles, -?-, -?-, -?-, -?-, -?-, Lizzie Isles, -?-, -?-, -?-, -?-, Billy Isles.

Pilling soldiers of the First World War. Wearing puttees and carrying cartridge cases, this group of six includes Adam Stafford (third from left) and William Cross (extreme right).

Mr R.H. Porter holds the reins of two horses drawing a smart trap which was in use in the 1900s. This is in the drive of Fluke Hall, home of the Gardner family, who were instrumental in building Pilling Dyke to keep out the sea.

St William's RC School, Pilling Moss, holds a concert, *c.* 1910. The barefoot girls pointing out a shipwreck on stormy seas are, left to right: Lizzie Hornby, Martha Brighouse, Elsie Curwen, Hannah Brighouse, May Ireton and Maggie Bryning.

The vicar of Pilling with his wife and daughter in the Vicarage rose gardens in the 1900s. The gardens were so well known that visitors included them with the Elleston's Arms bowling green at Stakepool in their sight-seeing.

Skippool Creek, now centred on a Marina for weekend yachtsmen as shown by this 1956 photograph, has a long history. Long before the port of Fleetwood was built there was a jetty for unloading at Skippool, a shipbuilding yard at nearby Wardleys and a customs house at Poulton-le-Fylde. Cargoes of flax and tallow were unloaded in the sixteenth century at these ancient ports, which served the whole Fylde coast. Hard gravelly shores enabled ships to unload and then refloat on the next tide if they anchored close to the banks. The seventeenth century saw considerable trade in tobacco, wines, timber and slate off the Fylde coast. In the mid-eighteenth century, ships from the West Indies came to Skippool with cargoes of sugar and slaves.

Hambleton Hall, also known as Ben Lewtas Cottage, photographed by J. Maynard Tomlinson in the 1920s, has a 1756 datestone over the door. Hambleton, a quaint hamlet of thatched, white-washed cottages, was the place from which the foolhardy attempted to cross the river at low tide, which led to fatalities.

Shard Bridge, Hambleton and the River Wyre, 1924. Since 1864 a favourite drive from Knott End was to Shard Bridge, returning by Wardleys Hotel to Stalmine and Preesall, a distance of 16 miles. Ten drives are listed in old guidebooks.

Fylde peat fire, 1940. Dick Higginson's wife is in her kitchen at Pilling. A peat fire gave off great heat but a large grate was necessary and had to have a correspondingly large ash hole. The disadvantage of burning peat was the fine ash left after burning – if disturbed, it floated all over the cottage.

Mrs Battersby and Mrs Scowcroft outside Beechcroft, Hambleton. These ladies gave voluntary instruction at the village sewing classes held in the school, which was built in 1880. Mrs Woodhouse of May Bank made Honiton lace, which was passed down as an heirloom. Fifty pieces of patchwork for a quilt could then be bought for 10d.

Lewtas family and housekeeper, 1873. Prosperous sons Matthew and Robert stand behind their parents. The largest ship built at Wardleys, the *Hope* (415 tons), was a Lewtas responsibility. Launching, under its commander John Cockbain, was one of the great days in North Fylde.

Hambleton peg mill, a drawing made in 1902 just before its demolition. James Baron, the miller, was known for miles around as he ground the finest flour. The advantage of this ancient peg or post mill was its capacity to be turned into favourable winds by simple rotation. To do this, a cart wheel attached to the post had to be manhandled. In course of time the peg wore out and could not be replaced, so the wooden mill was pulled down, a loss not only to bakers but to artists who came to Hambleton to draw or paint it. Local artist Charles Auty brought his students here, and one sketch by a civil engineer employed for a while on Fleetwood Docks actually travelled to St Petersburg.

Upper reaches of the River Wyre. The boundaries of the Fylde, when it was part of Amounderness, were not well defined. They stretched to Bowland Forest, an area which provided hunting man with rabbits, deer, grouse, fish and woodland birds.

# Acknowledgements

I am particularly grateful for help in compiling this book to John Higginson of Pilling, Charles Martland and Eddie Funk of Fleetwood, Mrs Christine Storey of the Poulton Historical Society and Mr Lawrenson of the Fylde Country Life Museum, all of whom have given generously of their time and talents.

To the many others who have supplied photographs and information I offer my sincere thanks and hope I have not overlooked anyone.

John Anderson • Fred Anyon • Charles Ashton • Miss M. Baron
Mr K. Beardmore • the late Dr T.S. Blacklidge
Braithwaite Manor Restaurant • H.J. Brown • Mr Buckley
Stanley Butterworth • Dr J.M. Canning • Carleton Community Group
Mr G. Cato • Martin Clegg • Anthony Coppin • A.E. Coppock
the late Charles Forrest Doughty • *Fleetwood Chronicle* • Mr E. Formstone
Mrs Gregory • J.R. Ingle • Isle of Man Steam Packet Company
Lancashire Library • *Lancashire Life* • Lancashire Museum • Jane Livesey
M.M. Loddington • Eric Mills • John Mollart • Joyce Morris
Miss Dorothy Nickson • Mrs Peers • Alice Penswick
Poulton Historical Society • Mrs Richard • Revd Dr E.J. Rothwell
the late Margaret Rowntree • Ron Severs • Mrs Sherlock • Ralph Smedley
D.B. Timms • *West Lancashire Evening Gazette* • Windsor Woollies
Miss D. Winterbotham • Mr G.R. Wood • Mr R. Wright.